KIWITOWN'S PORT

Gavin McLean

KIWITOWN'S PORT

THE STORY
OF
OAMARU HARBOUR

OTAGO

To my adopted family –
Ky, Vicky, Duchess and Croc

Published by

Otago University Press
PO Box 56 / Level 1, 398 Cumberland Street,
Dunedin, New Zealand

Fax: +64 3 479 8385
Email: university.press@otago.ac.nz
Website: www.otago.ac.nz/press

First published 2008
Copyright © Gavin McLean 2008
ISBN 978 1 877372 63 6

Book design by Ralph Lawrence

Published with the assistance of the History Group,
Ministry for Culture and Heritage

Printed through Condor Production Ltd,
Hong Kong

Page 1: Yacht at Holmes Wharf, December 2007.
– Gavin McLean

Pages 2–3: The trawler Aorere *glides into port*
under a hot North Otago sun.
– Gavin McLean

Above: Dinghies on the old slipway, December
2007. For generations fishermen used wooden
flatties to land their catch from boats moored in
the harbour. These days their contents are more
likely to be recreational fishing tackle, mates
and crates of beer. – Gavin McLean

Contents

OVERTURE

6

1: 'GOOD PLACE FOR BOATS EXCEPT DURING S.E. WINDS' 1840–1868

16

2: 'THE BREAKWATER AND NOTHING BUT THE BREAKWATER' 1868–1884

32

3: "WE'LL MEND THE BREAK, AND ... WE'LL PADDLE OUR OWN CANOE' 1885–1907

56

4: 'WE WILL DREDGE!' 1907–1940

76

5: 'A NAVIGATIONAL HAZARD' 1941–1974

96

6: 'FINGERS CROSSED ENGINEERING' 1975–2008

116

7: ENVOI: 'THERE'S NAUGHT TO FEAR FOR THE PORT OF OAMARU'

130

APPENDIX 1: HARBOUR TIMELINE *138*
APPENDIX 2: WRECKS AND ACCIDENTS *141*

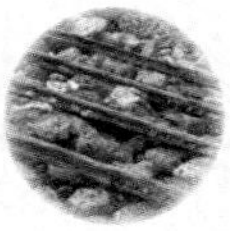

NOTES *146*
INDEX *148*
ACKNOWLEDGMENTS *152*

Overture

'Songs loud and long for our harbor board will
sweep across the sky.
What bold men dare, no jealousy can stop
what they will do,
They ventured and they quickly made a
port of Oamaru.'

Do not believe everything you see carved in stone. Out in Harbour Street as the thermometer grazed 30 degrees, workmen sweated away, putting the finishing touches to the old Oamaru Harbour Board offices. After a year's work, Dooley's stonemasons had given its crumbling façade an expensive heritage nip and tuck. Crowning their efforts was the reinstated soaring balustrade designed by Thomas Forrester for his employer. But the effect almost overwhelms such a narrow structure, and confirms historian Erik Olssen's canny comment that the grand facades of Oamaru's booster architecture disguise how little sometimes lay behind them. The reconstruction has added the dates 1876 (construction) and 2006 (restoration) to that 'big hair' balustrade, but the latter is a fib frozen in time, since in February 2007 it was still far from complete. But that was perhaps in keeping with its former owner. The archival trail left by the harbour board reveals that delays and frustrations were hardwired into its story.

The Victorians have gone, but the Pacific rolls on, periodically punching holes in the big breakwater the board put between the planet's mightiest ocean and their capitalist dreams. From the back windows of their old offices, I watched contractors clamping together giant steel moulds. A concrete truck lurked nearby, ready to fill another four-legged tetrahedron, or tetrapod as they are called, one of hundreds to come. At $1800 a pop (or pod), these wave deflectors are not cheap. Nor are they permanent. Along the breakwater's seaward side the eroding stumps of their predecessors slowly succumb to surf and surge. Just like everything else here.

I crossed the railway track, skirted the rusting grain silos and emerged at Friendly Bay. Near the entrance to Holmes Wharf, three youths, so brown they could only be backpackers, soaked up the sun, smoking and chatting gutturally. Before them lay the pacific Pacific. Today it was a topaz millpond languidly stirred by the very gentlest of swells. A small fishing boat was hove-to, cleaning its catch beneath a raucous, wheeling flock of gulls. Nothing lay between it and Chile. Like

Sacrificial warriors. As if on parade, tetrapods await transport to the breakwater, the latest recruits in Oamaru's battle against erosion. – Gavin McLean

Opposite: Harbour Street. In 1876 Thomas Forrester designed the masonry equivalent of a padded bra for his optimistic employers. The Oamaru Harbour Board was bullish and 'something of its confidence in the future of the port of Oamaru is expressed in the decorative exuberance of the façade of the Harbour Board building'. Conal McCarthy observed in Forrester and Lemon of Oamaru: Architects, the 'boldly projecting cornice', the 'vermiculated rustication of the voissoirs and quoins of the ground floor', which with Palladian-influenced window arches gave the building a Venetian air, entirely appropriate for the anticipated associations between Oamaru as a prosperous seaport and Venice as the maritime capital of Renaissance Europe.' Step inside, however, and you will see that there is barely enough room to swing a wharf rat – this wonderful old pile is all 'front'. The building (photographed in December 2007) now houses the Oamaru Whitestone Civic Trust's office. – Gavin McLean

everyone else, the young men were killing time before the penguin colony opened at dusk. On the other side of the mole, mothers watched over their boys splashing in the shallows of Friendly Bay, the harbour's pocket beach. Only the vibrant colours of the boys' Speedos and boardies, and the cell phone in one mum's ear, defined it as a twenty-first century scene.

From that tiny artificial beach I looked across the bay. A paint shop's test chart of yachts and pleasure launches glistened in the sun, their numbers increasing thanks to the economic boom and cheap mooring fees. Battered, smelly, but more interesting, fishing boats clustered along Holmes Wharf, where three generations ago giant 'Home boats' loaded wool and meat for Britain. On the other side of the harbour, Sumpter Wharf ran skeletally into the bay from the south. Now fenced off, it is shag heaven, the 'Oamaru bird dock' according to one Flickr contributor. Not far away, thousands more birds

conferenced on the breakwater, peeling off noisily in waves of feathers and frustration whenever tourists braved the old sea wall.

This is unmistakably Oamaru, yet it is also Everytown. Although the histories of the North and South Islands differ – something the northern authors of our national histories underplay – it exemplifies the 'rush to be rich' or the 'progress industry' that did more than North Island bush warfare to reshape New Zealand's destiny in the pivotal 1860s and 1870s. Oamaru played its part in that demographic and economic swamping. Nearly thirty years ago, geographer Kenneth Cumberland called Oamaru 'Kiwitown', the archetypal rural servicing town, manufacturing centre and port.[1] Viticulture, dairy units and farmstays are changing North Otago, but the land still produces, farmers still shop in Thames Street, factory whistles still sound knocking-off time, and the tides still roll in and out of the harbour.

Swimmers and rowers take to Friendly Bay as heat haze builds up off shore, February 2007. – Gavin McLean

sh and ships. Gulls wheel erhead as the Torea *surges to port, February 2007, a re survivor of the inshore hing fleet.* – Gavin McLean

Same old, same old? Not exactly, for the port is morphing into a heritage centre, recreation space and tourist venue. In this it is following a national trend. The big cities have jazzed up their waterfronts, sometimes barging in token heritage buildings. Kaiapoi and Wanganui operate restored heritage vessels, and Hokitika has a waterfront historical walk. Oamaru may have taken longer to wake up and smell the short black, but it holds a powerful hand. No other New Zealand town can match the richness and integrity of the wharves and buildings found here. The SUVs, cell phones and discarded McDonalds wrappers show that it is not quite the Victorian/Edwardian time capsule the costumed 'Living Victorians' who inhabit the historic precinct believe.

Small fishing boats nestle alongside Holmes Wharf, where Home boats once loaded frozen meat, wool and tallow for London. – Gavin McLean

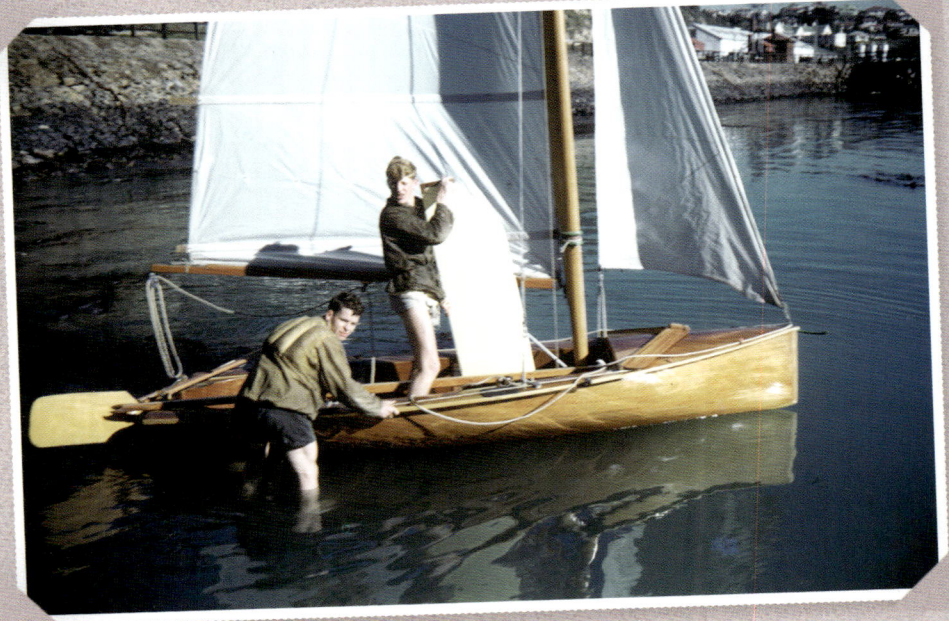

For youngsters growing up after World War II, Idle-Alongs such as 'Lyric', I.42, and other wooden yachts provided a taste of the briny. These photographs were taken by the North Otago Yacht and Power Boat Club's ramp by the old slipway beside Normanby Wharf. In the bottom image, notice the array of corrugated 'red sheds' in the background. The ones to the right survive today and are used by steam train operators and other heritage businesses, but the ramshackle one on the Cross Wharf behind 'Lyric's' sail, is long gone. – Graeme Ferris

Coasters in colour. The Kanna *(top)* and her sister Katui *made over 400 calls in the twenty years after the war. She is shown in the old 'collier' black hull that the Union Company replaced with bronze green from 1960. The elegant Dutch-built Holmwood (below) was an early postwar design, albeit anachronistic in clinging to the old 'three island' (bow, midships bridge and poop) model. – Grant Seath*

Shagged city. It took a while for nature to colonise the breakwater. Shags must have been a novelty a hundred years ago, because in May 1901 the Otago Witness *reported that one 'received a rather sudden surprise at Oamaru down at the breakwater' by being washed into the harbour by a big wave. After shaking itself and swimming for 100 metres, the bird flew off with only its dignity harmed. Raising the breakwater enhanced its attraction to the birds and they increased in numbers, so much so that by mid-century local fishermen were complaining about their effect on the fishery.* – Gavin McLean

Nevertheless it is easy to conjure up images of 'Moa', the world's second-biggest travelling steam crane, building the breakwater block-by-block, or the *Terra Nova's* boat crew rowing ashore stealthily in the dark to telegraph news of Captain Robert Falcon Scott's death in Antarctica, or 10,000-ton 'Home' boats loading for London.

In this pictorial essay we will explore the harbour's past and present. No need to have visited, for elements in this story will be familiar. Colonial New Zealand depended on sea transport. Every major or aspiring centre had to have a port. At different times, and with different casts of characters, similar stories were acted out throughout New Zealand. You can tick them off – from siting and building the port, right through to our modern worries about balancing the competing demands of conservation and development against those of commercial, recreational and residential users.

Kiwitown's Port: The Story of Oamaru Harbour mixes historic photographs and drawings with the evidence of the past that we fuzzily label 'heritage'. Although we have come to see the harbour as an historic place, the 1884 song that kicks off this overture is a reminder that it was once the stage on which our ancestors acted out their rush to be rich. Today's heritage object is yesterday's developer's vision. So we should also read these rotting piles, rusting chains and sagging sheds as footholds to the future.

Great dreams were once made here.

Chapter One

'GOOD PLACE FOR BOATS EXCEPT DURING S.E WINDS'[1]

Cape Wanbrow. The very name, given by explorer W.B. Mantell, suits the bland promontory brooding over the old business district and port area. It has changed a great deal since he clapped eyes on it, and not for the better if your desires run to nature in its pristine condition. The Cape as it is often called (though early Oamaruvians also called the tip South Head or the Point) suffers from the attentions of the generations of engineers who blasted rock from its northern edge to feed the harbour works and reclamations. But on sunny days when the changing play of light textures the great gashes carved out by their quarry, those gouges add character to the only 'interruption of any consequence to the long monotonous shoreline of low cliff and gravel beach which stretches 225 kilometres southwards from Banks Peninsula.'[2]

That is, of course, how the West sees things. Those whiskery Victorians frozen in formal studio portraits like Jurassic ants in amber landed here as young, hard-as-nails merchants, farmers and sailors. They measured the quality of a coast by the degree of shelter it offered ships. The first colonists, the Eastern Polynesians who evolved into Maori, would have seen things differently. They would have welcomed some shelter when running before a southerly, but canoes did not need deepwater anchorages. For that reason, Oamaru with its puny little creek had less pulling power than the great food-rich river mouths on either side of it, the Shag (Waihemo) and Waitaki. There Maori harvested on near-industrial scale.

We still debate the origins of the name Oamaru. It is most often said to mean 'the place of Maru.' But who was Maru? Some say a god, others a person. Another common translation is 'a sheltered place'. Herries Beattie, on the other hand, linked the name to the legend that Oamaru stone was the solidified form of Tamatea's fire. While journeying north, explorer and carrier of fire, Tamatea, dropped the sacred bark container carrying the fire, which sank into the earth and is said to have been preserved for many years as an underground burning seam of coal.[3]

Cape Wanbrow, from which the picture on the previous two pages was taken, rises above Oamaru's eroding foreshore. The winter 2007 storms made the national news by demolishing part of a joinery factory and exposing the wooden bracing erected in the late 1930s to hold the old steam engines and concrete blocks dumped to protect the foreshore. It is an ancient struggle: six thousand years ago the coastline was four kilometres further out to sea.
– *Gavin McLean*

Water, not fire, now shapes North Otago's coastline. The volcanoes have been silent for millions of years, but the coast around Oamaru is still dynamic. Listen to the surf breaking on the beach one calm night and you will hear the restless, relentless Pacific winning its ancient battle with the land. Millions of years ago, when shallow seas broke over coastal Otago, the schist core was covered by layers of sandstones, limestones and mudstones. Over time the land rose, to give us the fields, down-lands and gentle hills that define North Otago. In geological terms, though, this is a mere loan, as the sea is attacking these softer rocks and is reclaiming its old dominion.[4] In even the short span of a single human lifetime you can watch some of this ancient drama being acted out. In her novel *The Edge of the Alphabet*, Janet Frame's character Toby Withers reflects on the sea: 'A near thin stretch of menace pounding loosening the rocks of the wall which the Town Council keeps reinforcing, knowing that in the end the Pacific Ocean will triumph and surge across the railway lines over the engine-sheds and the station platform and the offices and the road.' Toby is convinced that 'the sea will triumph',[5] but it still has a way to go, despite talk of global warming and rising sea levels. Who knows?

Our eyes can see cliffs and beaches, but not the seabed. Few people know that Cape Wanbrow marks an interesting break in the composition of the seafloor. To the south, it is sand; north of the Cape, it is shingle. In the days before modern electronic navigation devices, fishermen sounded with the traditional lead line when coming in at night or in thick fog: 'If we got a bit astray and came in on the shingle, you knew you were north of Oamaru', fisherman Syd Tangney recalled.[6]

Shingle or sand, both are recycled land. Overall, the coasts here are retreating, in places rapidly, adding to the sediment discharged by the Clutha and Waitaki rivers into the longshore drift.[7] Already the bill has been high. In the nineteenth century, Oamaru's first woollen mill and

the playing grounds of Waitaki Boys' High School were swept away. A hundred years later, the threat reasserts itself periodically. North of the town, just past the rock walls that protect its heart more successfully than Toby allowed, is the start of that vast horizon of rampart-like shingle beaches that stretch north up the Canterbury coast with few interruptions. 'The sound of surf crashing into the berm of these cobble beaches and draining back into the sea is unforgettably loud, reflecting the energy dissipated on these beaches.'[8] No need to tell that to the marine engineers who have struggled to protect port and town for 150 years. In the winter of 2007, a hungry swell swallowed twenty metres of coastline in a few days, claiming a joinery company's premises just north of the rock walls.

Who settled here, if Maori shunned the harbour for more protected shores? Whalers knew of Oamaru, although they preferred Moeraki and Otago Harbour. So did surveyors. In 1844 that peppery surveyor, Frederick Tuckett, seeking a site for the Scottish colony, dismissed Oamaru as inferior to Moeraki, but chose Dunedin. The town's European phase finally began in 1853, when Hugh Robison built a hut there on the edge of Run 15. What did the place look like? The waves broke against Cape Wanbrow, which then ran straight down into the sea. On the southern edge of the small plain on which the town would emerge, a few cabbage trees poked their fronds above the little lagoons, flax, matagouri, fern and spear-grass. Near the edge of the Cape, a stream – so insignificant it is still known simply as the 'Oamaru Creek' – twisted and turned towards the sea, entering a murky lagoon behind a shingle beach before wandering another kilometre south and finally entering the sea near the Cape.

The runholders depended on the sea for everything. The first ship known to have worked cargo off the beach was the schooner *Endeavour* in January 1854, which

The frail lifeline. Oamaru depended on the landing service's open boats, seen here following the guide wires to the exposed beach. The boatmen were a tough breed who could be relied on to help whenever ships got into trouble. Many merchants, however, disliked the slow, costly service and the fact that its owners sometimes favoured their own business interests. In October 1870, for example, 'Free Trade' alleged that 'other merchants, shipowners, and business people outside the clique, would be subject to loss and inconvenience if they happen to come into collision with their operations.' – North Otago Museum 4192

took twenty-one bales of wool to Dunedin. The trouble, as the early voyages that followed showed, was that the Cape gave little protection from easterlies. So, although trade grew steadily, cautious mariners worked cargo off Oamaru by day and sheltered overnight at Moeraki. In the four years between 1854 and 1858, a handful of tiny craft – mostly the *Ann Jane, Star* and *Spec* – linked Oamaru to Dunedin and ports as far south as the Molyneux. They brought in 'stores for settlers' and took out between four and thirty-two bales of wool, all laboriously boated out to the anchored ships.

Little could be done to improve this doubtful haven. The Otago provincial government ran the harbours, but could barely develop Otago Harbour at its doorstep, let alone the outports, all cawing for wharves, jetties and pilot stations like hungry chicks in a nest. In 1858 it built a derrick to hoist goods from the landing area, and a goods store, and advertised for a manager for the boating service. In November the 'government store', 'a frame building, boarded and roofed with Hobart Town palings', opened for business. It was run by the former Moeraki trader H.C. Hertslett, who advised that goods 'must be addressed in

full.' It was a post office as much as a storehouse.[9]

From 1860, the landing site was also served by James Hassell, Charles Traill and Eustace Roxby, who from August advertised themselves as surfboat proprietors, wool brokers and agents. They built a store capable of holding 1500 bales of wool. The most important newcomer, however, was Captain William Sewell, who also set up a new boating service. He arrived on 13 October 1860 and would dominate Oamaru's maritime affairs until he retired as harbourmaster thirty-six years later. Sewell's two surfboats and eight crew were deemed 'a great improvement' on the service offered by Tom Hardy's sole boat, and started a new round of competition, in which Hardy brought three boats and thirty Maori boatmen up from Moeraki.

The final 'improvement' of 1860 was the arrival of the brig *Thomas and Henry*, bought in November by a government that in this act compounded its stinginess with dimwittedness. Why Dunedin's tyro politicians wanted to moor an immobile hulk off a killer beach was a mystery, and what good it did to anyone was equally perplexing to Oamaruvians. No one would have been happier than hulk keeper William Hay, when his precarious perch was towed away early in April 1861. The settlers were almost as glad. Many years later, one described the hulk as 'utterly useless for any purpose whatever' and recalled that 'the disappearance of the black, ungainly object that had floated on the water, the scoff and jest of all the sailing masters who visited the port, was a relief to the eye.'[10]

At least the derrick and the government store did some good. A wharf to serve them would have been even more useful. Tenders for building one were invited in the *Otago Witness* of 11 December 1858, but the prices must have been too high for Dunedin's misers, for next year the paper was still bemoaning Oamaru's harbour facilities as the worst in the province. The *Witness* considered

this scandalous for 'the outlet for a large extent of our finest sheep country, and our frontier upon our Northern boundary'. Then the provincial engineer proposed a screw-pile jetty 'at a sufficient height above the water to be out of the reach of the surf', but again the £3000–£4000 price was too much for the government.[11]

So people relied on surfboats. 'A stout hawser rope through slots at the bow and stern of a boat called the tender which was moored several chains off-shore, was secured to stanchions above the beach,' G.L. Grenfell recalled in the 1930s. 'A surf boat returning from a vessel arrived alongside the hawser and the bow oarsman would ship his oar and secure the hawser with a short boathook and hold the bow until the other oarsman had swung the boat bow to seaward.' When that was done, the men shipped the hawser into slots at the bow and stern, and began hauling the boat hand over hand until the bow grounded on the beach. On shore, the boat was firmly secured to the hawser, so that its bow remained afloat. By now it was surrounded by boatmen, who waded out to unload its contents. Once the boat had been emptied, the boatmen grasped the hawser, their colleagues gave a firm push-off and the crew returned to the tender, where they cast off the hawser and rowed to the ship to load more cargo.[12] It was wet, sweaty, dangerous work. People came ashore in the same way and the final indignity for passengers was scaling the steep bank above the landing place with the help of a rope.

Logs and sawn timber were floated ashore in improvised bundles and rafts. In *The Boy-Colonists*, E. Simeon Elwell caught the adventure of it. When young Harry and Ernest reached Oamaru to unload sawn timber, they were given striped shirts and moleskin trousers and told to leave their other clothes on the beach. 'The mode of landing the timber was like this', Elwell recalled:

> The sailors fastened many planks together, making them into small rafts; these they lowered over the side, and tossed some

Hansbeck Street Oamaru about

The sailor's friend. In the early days, the first Northern Hotel (centre, with flagpole) was a welcome beacon for seafarers and for passengers arriving in Oamaru. The old hotel's 1873 limestone replacement still occupies the same site, albeit looking a little shabby. – North Otago Museum 194

and paddled others to the shore as far as they would float. As soon as the rafts had grounded, Harry and Ernest had to dash into the water, mount them, let go the fastenings, and then secure as best they might the scattered and floating planks. The sea was rather rough that day, and as the beach shelves very suddenly, they had no very easy and very safe task. Often just as they commenced loosening the knot, a big wave would wash right over them, raft and all. Mr J. joined vigorously in the work. He was fully up to everything of the kind, and well able to direct all hands, having in early days been accustomed to a great deal of the same kind of work. About every two hours he went round with a bottle of rum, giving each hand a small 'nip', as it was called. Harry took his share, but Ernest did not like spirits, and found he got on equally well or better without them. At twelve o'clock they 'knocked off' for dinner, which they ate as they were, in their wet clothes. The smokers then took a pipe, but Harry and Ernest went on with their work. Once or twice, venturing too far, they almost got carried away, for, though the water was not deep, the beach was so steep and the shingle afforded so uncertain a footing that even in the shallowest water as the waves retired it was almost impossible to keep one's feet.[13]

The first steam ships appeared off the beach in 1859: the *Queen* (January) and the *Pirate* and *Geelong*

(February). Steam power liberated ships from the tyranny of wind and tide and made it possible to plan travel arrangements with confidence. In August, the *Geelong* began a subsidised fortnightly service. By the late 1860s she was running twice-weekly, supplemented by the smaller *Wallace*. It was a four-hour journey to Timaru and five hours to Dunedin.

In an age before railways and reliable roads, people watched the comings and goings in their harbours as attentively as we monitor cars in a suburban cul de sac. When the Harbour Steam Company's 'handsome' steamer *Maori* first visited under the command of 'the well-known and deservedly highly-esteemed' Captain Malcolm, for example, she announced her arrival by firing a gun. The Northern Hotel replied by running the ensign up its flagpole. While this was going on, the *Wallace* steamed around the point. 'As she passed the aboriginal [Maori] she fired a gun, which had, one would think,

been specially charged for the occasion, as the detonation fairly shook the buildings opposite.' The Northern Hotel seems to have liked putting out the welcome mat. When the *Tararua* called in October 1870 for wool, for example, the hotel flew the Union Steam Ship Co flag and Oamaruvians rowed out to inspect her, while her passengers looked over their town.[14]

One day in October 1869, three steamers were in 'the Roads': the *Maori*, *Wallace* and *Beautiful Star*. As the first two were fixed to sail at the same time, 'a race was looked to, and a considerable number of persons assembled to witness the start, and a few ventured bets on the event.' The bigger, lightly laden *Maori* had the advantage. The *Wallace* was handicapped by being down by the head and listing to port, but the ships slipped their anchors at 1136 and 1138 hours respectively and passed the Point at 1146 and 1147, trailing thick clouds of smoke, watched by a big crowd.[15] Sadly for posterity – though not surprising, given the injunctions against racing – the paper did not report the result.

All too often, people looked out not at triumphs, but at wreckage. Oamaru Bay was a dangerous place. The month of the *Maori–Wallace* race, the newspaper reported a common problem. The schooner *Dagmar*, which had just arrived in the Roads, had put to sea with the Onehunga. 'On Wednesday night both vessels were tacking about in the offing, the signal "Keep to sea" being still hoisted,

and in the afternoon stood in to the southward. They will probably have run into Moeraki.'[16]

The Oamaruvians of the 1860s saw that signal run up the flagstaff too often for their liking. The first casualty occurred in October 1860, when the schooner *Oamaru Lass* was wrecked; she was refloated and renamed *Nora*. In 1862, four ships got into trouble in the bay: the schooner *Wellington* and brigantine *Robert and Betsy* were lost and the schooners *Star of Tasmania* and *Brisk* were recovered. Things were quiet until 1865, when the *Gazehound* was lost at the port.

Mariners knew not to linger off the town. In November 1866, the *Oamaru Times and Waitaki Reporter* got twitchy over delays to the barque *Royal Bride*, which had brought cargo from London a month earlier. There had been disputes between the captain and the seamen, some of whom had tried to escape in the ship's boat before being threatened with a gun. 'Four of them are now in gaol for insubordination; two more are ill with scurvy,

Fallen flagship. 'We regret to have to report the wreck of the pride of the port—the Premier, *an almost-new vessel', the* North Otago Times *reported on 1 August 1871. About midnight a couple of days earlier the much feared 'black nor-easter' set in. The Oamaru-owned* Premier *slipped her cable but the wind lulled, leaving her at the mercy of the heavy seas, which proved too strong for her anchors. Captain Herman Bouman was exonerated. – North Otago Museum*

while the remaining men refuse duty', it reported, siding with the captain. It also blamed 'great mismanagement in the stowage of the cargo', mixing up the Oamaru and Invercargill goods. But the paper was clearly more worried that the port's reputation would suffer if the ship was blown ashore before new crew could be recruited: 'The name of the port must not suffer through such a contingency.'[17]

The *Royal Bride* got away safely, and 1866 ended without a single wreck. That run of luck ended on 13 March 1867, when the *Vixen* and *Stately* went ashore. A heavy sea was running and Captain Sewell ordered the

ships to 'stand to sea'. Two ignored him. The *Vixen* hit the beach broadside-on, but rescuers fastened lines to each mast and kept her upright. Captain Thomas Short had thought the *Stately* safe at the moorings, but that evening she started to drift. At 2300 hours he set all sail, but the wind failed, and at around midnight the *Stately* hit the rocks south of the landing place. Next day, Sewell, Short and another master ruled out salvaging the three-month-old schooner.

The *Vixen* was hauled off the beach on 4 April in an operation that set the pattern for all future jobs. Workmen built wooden launching ways and removed rocks and

'WHEN CAPTAIN EDIE'S SHIP MAKES
ANOTHER PLEASURE TRIP'

The Dunedin–Oamaru steamers were household names in settler
Oamaru, essential lifelines for travel to and from Dunedin and the
ports between. At times they also offered welcome holiday excursions,
as this report in the Oamaru Times *for*
12 November 1869 shows:

Tuesday last being the Prince of Wales's birthday, all the business establishments were closed, and all Oamaru and Moeraki gave themselves up to holiday-making. The p.s. *Wallace*, which was gaily dressed in flags, took down a large number of excursionists from Oamaru, including the fife and drum band of No. 8 Company, arriving at Moeraki about half-past 12 o'clock. The day was a very favourable one for outdoor enjoyment, there being a pleasant breeze, while the clouded sky protected from the inconvenience of too ardent a sun. The wind being nearly dead astern, the *Wallace* went down at a spanking pace, and although there was a little sea on, very few of the passengers appeared to suffer from that 'bete noir' of voyageurs, the mal-de-mer. Perhaps this was greatly owing to the fact that the lively strains of the band, which played for a succession of quadrilles, polkas, schottisches, and even waltzes, gave everybody something better to do than to contemplate the water, pocket-handkerchief in hand. It was not the least part of the enjoyment of those who, not content to play the part of mere spectators, themselves tripped the light fantastic too, that the gentle rolling of the vessel ever and anon made it just sufficiently difficult to keep their balance, to add a spice of fun to the relish of the dancing itself. Some little difficulty, in consequence of the shallowness of the water – it being quite low tide – was experienced in bringing the steamer alongside the jetty, warping having to be resorted to, the operation causing a delay of some twenty minutes.

The jetty was thronged with visitors from Hampden, Otepopo, and Moeraki, who greeted the steamer with hearty cheers. The debarkation having been accomplished by the aid of strong helping hands which lifted the passengers one by one from the paddle-box to the jetty, a step of about three feet, hand-shakings and cordial greetings were pretty generally exchanged; as everybody seemed to know, and be on the best terms with everybody. Even the Maories [sic], of whom there must have been fully a hundred present, some on the jetty and others grouped in every variety of position on the hillside, seemed to participate in the general enjoyment. A number of them watched the dancing in the shed which was soon begun to the strains of the Oamaru Band, with evident interest, and many a dark-eyed waihena [sic] showed her white teeth as she laughingly looked on at the way in which the Pakehas amused themselves. And all did that, and despite the opinion of Frenchmen, as to English custom, there was not on this occasion an atom of ground for the remark 'S'amusaient tristement.' While some were dancing in the large and pleasant shed, wherein was a capital floor for the purpose, and which being

open at the sides allowed all to see and be seen; others went away in little groups to roam among the bush or on the level sandy beach, while an indefatigable few went as far as the Maori Kaik to have a look at the houses of the dark-skinned inhabitants of Moeraki. As we were not of that few, we must postpone a description of the kaik till our next trip. About two o'clock the s.s. *Maori*, bringing another batch of excursionists from Dunedin, and Mons Fleury's capital Brass band, arrived; but not being able to get alongside the jetty, had to land her passengers in small boats, so that the last of them did not get ashore until nearly if not quite three o'clock. The Dunedin Band proved a great acquisition, and about four o'clock relieved the Oamaru band, which had kept the dancers going up till that time. A number of the passengers per *Wallace*, were at half past one o'clock, entertained by the captain at a very handsome dejeuner provided on board. The tasteful style in which the viands, of which there was an unsparing abundance, were served up, and the whole arrangement of the table did the greatest credit to the ship's steward, Mr F.D. Lawrenson. After the more solid refreshment had been done ample justice to, the health of captain Edie, proposed by Mr Steward in suitable terms, was drunk with musical honours, and the party then left the ship to make the most of the remaining time on shore.

We should not forget to mention here that Mr Leggatt was most kind and attentive to the visitors, keeping open house, and if anyone had not plenty to eat and drink it was certainly not his fault. At five o'clock a gun was fired as a signal to embark, and Mr Leggatt called for three cheers for the visitors, which were heartily given, as were also three cheers for Moeraki in response thereto. Then all embarked on board the *Wallace*, which carried the Dunedin visitors to the Maori, and in a few minutes both vessels were steaming merrily away, bands playing and colors flying, on the return trip, which passed off as pleasantly and happily as the passage down. The *Wallace* arrived at Oamaru about 8.00 p.m. and landed her passengers, who all seem to have thoroughly enjoyed the day, and among whom the one sentiment seemed to have prevail[ed].

> *'When Captain Edie's ship*
> *Makes another pleasure trip*
> *May we 'be there to see,'*

As Cowper says of Johnny Gilpin's ride. Mr Murcott of the Hampden Hotel had a bar in Mr Leggatt's old store, and also, with wise forethought, a room for the lady visitors, where 'the cup that cheers but not inebriates,' in the shape of tea and coffee, was dispensed.

boulders from the beach before sliding the ship back in the water. Supervised by Sewell, the *Vixen* slid down the ways, surprising workmen by her speed, but they slewed her head around, to the cheers of onlookers. 'The smiles that came over the countenances of the owners on board, as their vessel went off into deep water, sufficiently testified to the state of their feelings on the occasion.'[18]

Accidents like this played into the hands of those who wanted to make Moeraki the port for North Otago. In 1866, however, the provincial government finally awarded the tender for a wooden L-shaped jetty at Oamaru, designed by J.M Balfour. It must have been in an uncharacteristically generous mood, as it ordered a timber-decked jetty on iron piles, the costliest of three options explored.

Dunedin contractor Hugh Calder commenced work in November 1865 and the foundation stone was laid in December. The work was plagued by delays. After three months, Calder had to stop work to wait for wrought iron piles to arrive from Scotland. A dispute with the supervising engineer stopped work from December 1866 to April 1867, but within months of its resumption Traill, Roxby & Co's crane was loading stone from the incomplete jetty.

But would it last? The jetty jutted out from Cape Wanbrow, at a place known as the Point, where it was completely exposed. Local critics had called the site pure folly, but Provincial Treasurer Julius Vogel's comment that if it was too vulnerable it should be abandoned and replaced by the railway to Moeraki stilled their tongues. Second best was better than nothing. The *Oamaru Times* came out swinging: 'The money voted for it was, as it were, wrenched out of Government fingers, and ever since it cannot but have been manifest that the Oamaru Jetty works have been regarded as Oamaru's sugar-plum – a bauble given to her to keep her quiet'.

So the *Oamaru Times* grasped at straws, seeing the jetty's survival in the *Vixen* and *Stately* storm as 'convincing proof of the feasibility of converting the exposed roadsteads of New Zealand, at a trifling expenditure of treasure, into safe and available harbors.'[19] It preferred to blame shipmasters for every incident, unwilling to contemplate the port being at fault. Thus it castigated the *Stately's* master for ignoring orders to put to sea. It also welcomed the provincial harbourmaster's promise to provide thicker mooring cables and tougher regulations. Thomson threatened to take away the licences of masters who ignored instructions to leave the anchorage. Acknowledging that some people thought the *Stately's* master acted correctly in trusting to the moorings, the *Times* nevertheless concluded that 'the moorings have been found shamefully insecure'.[20]

There were two sets of moorings. The inner ones, for smaller craft, had been laid in 1862 in 5.5 metres of water 400 metres from the beach. Many ships used them. The outer moorings, for ships of up to 700 tons, were a mile and a half from the beach in water 9.1 metres deep. Few ships used them. Captain Thomson blamed this on shipmasters' concerns to make a quick getaway if the weather cut up rough suddenly. To save time and avoid the trouble of securing to the outer moorings, masters usually relied on their anchors.[21] In any case, the moorings were not perfect. The buoys parted sometimes and had to be recovered by the pilot schooner. In the six months to 31 March 1867, only the *Star of Tasmania* and *A.W. Stevens* used the outer moorings, which were removed in 1869.

But back to 1867. In the early hours of Monday 31 July, a south-easterly gale swept mountainous seas in the roadstead. Sewell flew the Blue Peter to order ships out to sea. Only the *Coquette* complied. A second signal sent the *Mary Ann Christina*, *Vixen*, *Edward* and *Christopher and Anne* scurrying, but the *Vistula*, *Midlothian* and *Hope* decided to ride out the storm. It was a costly mistake.

The *Midlothian* drifted towards the beach, her sails hopelessly split by the wind. Fortunately, her master ran her ashore undamaged on a sandy part of the beach. Then at 0530 hours the Auckland brigantine *Vistula* parted her cables and drifted ashore. She seems to have been incompetently commanded. Captain Paton was below, and all hands except the cook were asleep when the ship broke loose. He had stayed put, believing that he did not have sufficient ballast to sail safely. The *Oamaru Times* criticised 'the vessel being allowed to come ashore without shaking out a sail.'[22] During the morning Sewell tried to pull her bow into the waves, but after her rotten cables broke he left her to her fate. Miraculously, she survived her pummelling and later in the afternoon shore crews pulled her upright and started taking off cargo. By the time the *Hope* went ashore, the gale was moderating. She stranded opposite the Northern Hotel, undamaged. At one stage there were fears that wreckage seen floating in the bay came from another vessel, but it turned out to be

only the staging for the nearly finished jetty, cut loose to prevent it from damaging the wharf. Next morning there was almost another casualty when the steamer *Wainui*, entering the bay, got among the breakers and was worked out only with difficulty.

No lives had been lost and none of the ships was badly damaged. Even so, three ships resting unhappily on the beaches was a bad advertisement for Oamaru. And it was about to get worse. At 2330 on 14 August, the schooner *Banshee*, fresh from Hokitika to load potatoes, broke her cables and drove ashore nearly opposite the flagstaff, joining the *Vistula*, *Midlothian* and the *Hope*.

The only ones to benefit from their misfortune were the labourers who built the launching ways to salvage the wrecks. They raced against time, especially for the *Vistula*, whose damage was worse than originally thought. 'She is bulged ahead of the mainmast and will, we conceive, hardly pay for launching,' the *Oamaru Times* said on 20 August.[23] While the *Vistula*'s fate hung in the balance, the other ships were recovered. On 21 August, the *Midlothian* was warped out by fixed anchor. On 25 September, the *Hope* came off the beach, leaky, but able to limp to Otago Harbour.

That left the *Vistula* and the *Banshee*. Both were living on borrowed time, since auctioneer Henry France had sold them as wrecks on 13 September for £105 and £290 respectively. But their new owners were willing to take a chance, buoyed by seeing the *Midlothian* and *Hope* cheat death. They would use the steamer *Geelong* to tow them free. She was hooked up to the *Vistula*, but then diverted to the *Banshee* because the former ship's launching ways were not quite finished. It seemed that luck was against them. The *Banshee* moved only a few metres before sticking on shingle deposited by the waves. Was this the end? The *Geelong*'s master was keen to sail, for he had a mail and passenger contract to keep, but the unusually fine weather and the diplomacy of the salvors persuaded him to stay overnight for another try next morning. They were rewarded at high water on 28 September. The *Banshee* grounded temporarily on sand but was wrenched free by the *Geelong*, surprisingly undamaged for a ship abandoned to the underwriters. She sailed for Port Chalmers that day.[24]

Now only the *Vistula* was left. On 24 October she slid easily down the ways to the low water mark, where she stuck fast, resisting every effort by the *Geelong*. Captain Sewell's workers tried to bring her head around, but the warp broke. Since the tide was falling, the *Geelong* blew off steam to wait till high tide next day, when she again failed, barely moving the *Vistula*. They failed again a couple of days later. In desperation they pushed her on to her broadside to float her free, but she remained stuck and the *Geelong* gave up.[25] The *Vistula* broke up soon after.

Oamaru from the Cape in the
1860's, looking down on the
landing site. Note the signal
station and hut above the beach
– North Otago Museum 3238

The beach did not stay clear of wrecks for long. The brig *Highlander* had arrived from New South Wales with coal in time for the crew to watch the *Geelong* making a last effort at pulling off the *Vistula*. Soon it was their turn. On Sunday afternoon, 3 November, the *Highlander* flew her ensign upside-down, a distress sign. Oamaruvians flocked to the jetty and the esplanade to watch the drama as captain and crew rowed to the cutter *Hope*, anchored nearby, leaving the *Highlander* drifting towards the Cape. Observers criticised the crew for abandoning her so soon – only one anchor was down, and her yards appeared 'trimmed in such a manner as would facilitate her driving ashore'. After Sewell took out another anchor, the *Highlander*'s crew returned and lowered the distress signal. Towards evening the wind turned to the south, enabling her to anchor safely.

The affair seemed fishy, at least to the *Oamaru Times*, which observed pointedly that this 'very old vessel' was insured for £1200 whereas 'competent judges' gave £600 as 'her outside value'. 'Her cargo is also insured; and obviously, therefore, her owners would not lose by her becoming a wreck.' Returning to a familiar theme, the paper called for a searching inquiry 'as it is too bad that the character of the port should be prejudiced to suit the convenience of shipowners.'[26]

Had Oamaru's notoriety attracted ship wreckers, or was the paper being too defensive? We will never know. No inquiry was conducted into the behaviour of the captain and crew on 3 November. They remained aboard their ship, which lay in the roadstead. Seventeen days later a north-easterly gale scattered the shipping. The *Highlander* 'with great difficulty wore the point', and returned next day to continue unloading. Then, on Friday 22 November another north-easterly sent heavy rollers crashing into the bay. At 1100 the *Highlander* dragged her anchor, 'and after several ineffectual attempts to wear ship', went ashore 200 metres from the jetty. The crew escaped, but the old tub broke up.

Two days later, to cap off a miserable week, 'the sea rolled in with a violence seldom seen at Oamaru, great rollers every now and then washing clean over the jetty'. At 1700 hours the schooner *Caroline* hit the shore at the same spot as the *Vistula*. She had been shipping water since 1000. Captain Williams would have liked to have put to sea, but sails shredded by the wind forced him to trust to his anchors. Incredibly, they held, but at 1500 a wave swept away the skylight and stove in the front of the poop. That was it. When soundings revealed water in the hold, Williams ran ashore to save life. One man was dragged under the ship by a receding wave and would have been swept out to sea, had bystanders not intervened.

The bystanders were part of this drama, and one paid with his life. Surfboat crewman Daniel McLeod, originally from Scotland, was watching events from the beach with a friend, when a wave swept McLeod into the boiling sea and nearly did the same to his mate. McLeod swam to a wharf fender, and climbed half-way up before being plucked off by a wave. A good swimmer, he grabbed a rope and was several times hauled within metres of safety before a huge wave snatched him away for good. The seas also smashed two surfboats and almost claimed a third.

The events of the day were sobering. The *Oamaru Times* was still inclined to blame the shipowners and their captains: 'had the vessel [the *Caroline*] been properly found in sails this catastrophe would not have occurred.' But a new note of doubt had crept into its columns. Dunedin should have provided lifebuoys, but Sunday's events were a warning that a protective sea wall was necessary. 'Another storm or two like this and we may expect the whole structure to come ashore.'[27] How prophetic. It took just two months to happen. The storm that swept the coast on 3–4 February 1868 was yet another storm said to be of unprecedented fury. It may well have been, for howling east-south-east winds and

pouring rain flooded rivers from South Otago to North Canterbury, inundating farmland, drowning isolated settlers, wrecking bridges, buildings and ships.

Four ships were in the bay when Captain Sewell ran up the Blue Peter: the wool ships *Star of Tasmania* and *Water Nymph*, ketch *Otago* and schooner *Emu*. The *Star of Tasmania* had been calling at Oamaru for years to load for London. Before the day was out, four of the twenty-two men, women and children aboard – the two Baker children and seamen David Petrie of Arbroath, and Londoner William Brookes – would die in Oamaru's worst maritime disaster. The *Water Nymph*, laid down as a corvette for the French Navy, had been finished in 1855 as a merchant ship.

As always, it was easier for the smaller craft to escape. At 1330, half an hour after seeing the signal, the *Emu* worked out, followed thirty minutes later by the *Otago*. To Sewell's consternation, the larger ships did not stir. It was later discovered that the *Star* could not make out the signals, a double misfortune, since she blocked the *Water Nymph's* escape. At 1530 he again signalled 'proceed to sea without delay', but to no effect. The big ships were doomed.

The *Star of Tasmania* went first. With a portentous crack, her anchor cable snapped, sending her drifting until she was pulled up by the government moorings. She had broken them on an earlier visit, so no one was surprised when they snapped in mid-afternoon. The *Star* drifted about 500 metres before Captain William Culbert dropped the starboard anchor and the crew fished up the broken chain and dropped the other anchor again. They held briefly, then parted with a jolt, sending the big ship shorewards.

It was too dangerous to hoist sail. The huge rollers sweeping the decks were tossing the deck cargo about, making it suicidal to work there, so the crew climbed into the rigging. At 1900 hours the *Star of Tasmania* hit broadside-on, her head pointing south. 'The vessel rolled to and fro upon the shingle, and being heavily laden, strained and creaked as the enormous masses of water struck her and knocked her about,' a reporter wrote. 'Wave after wave leaped clean over her, and the vessel finally fell over on her port side, her masts quickly afterwards falling into the sea.'[28]

The flagstaff in the photograph on page 29 is the most tangible legacy of Oamaru's shipwreck past. It is a mast from the Robert and Betsy, *wrecked at the port in 1862. After serving as the port's signal mast, it spent decades in a Tyne Street garden before being refurbished and re-erected near the harbour slipway.*
– Gavin McLean

Passengers and crew crawled through the waves and spray to the starboard bow, Culbert leaping from the *Star's* battered poop just as it broke up. But this was no place to linger. The seas crashing over the *Star* were flinging cargo and wreckage about and the ship was falling apart. They had to get off, and quickly.

But how? Although the ship was only ten to twelve metres from shore, the wind, shrieking at gale force, flung back every rope tossed towards her. After watching these efforts fail, in desperation Stevens, the mate, leaped from the forecastle and struck for shore. Onlookers saw him disappear, only to re-emerge when a wave receded. He was about to be struck by another, bristling with timber and debris, when bystanders rushed in and dragged him ashore. They timed it perfectly – the sea was sucking at their feet as they raced to safety. Their elation was tempered by dismay at his having lost hold of the line he was carrying in the surf. Two more crewmen followed him ashore, but the next two drowned. One, caught in the undertow, was swept out to sea. Shocked by this, onlookers shouted to the people still aboard to wait for a line.

But what line? Boatman George McKenzie, who had been trying to get one aboard, had collapsed exhausted. Police sergeant Bullen waded into the surf, a rope around his waist, but his line hit the forecastle only once and on that occasion a wave swept it away before anyone could grab it. Captain Steward of the Volunteers fired a rocket gun he had improvised, a stout fishing line fired from a rifle, but the line kept parting from the ramrod.

Then McKenzie resumed his efforts, which were finally rewarded at 2240 when the rope hit the *Star's* deck and a crewman seized it. Minutes later boatman Duncan Young clambered aboard to loud cheers. Stevens followed, returning carrying a boy. One by one, the passengers and crew came ashore.

Stevens returned for Mrs Baker, slung her over his shoulder and 'commenced descending the life-line with his burden, but just as he reached the water an immense

This little hut is another much-travelled survivor. Once sited at the base of the flagstaff, and later the watchman's hut, after many adventures and moves, it now reposes in the former Oamaru Harbour Board building's back yard, awaiting restoration. – Gavin McLean

his burden, but just as he reached the water an immense wave dashed over the vessel and hid them for a moment from view. As the wave retired Stevens was seen hanging to the rope with Mrs Baker still clinging to him. Again a wave submerged them, and it was feared that they must both be carried away, but on its subsidence they were found to still be safe and in a few moments Stevens had got near enough to grasp the helping hands held out to him, and the lady and her preserver were brought safely ashore amid loud cheers.' According to the paper, her first words were 'Never mind me, save the poor, dear Captain'. Last off was Duncan Young who plunged ashore, cheered by hundreds, just as a wave retired.

Attention now swung to the other wool ship. About half an hour after the *Star* struck, the *Water Nymph*, closer to the shore, and previously hemmed in by the *Star*, started dragging her anchor. Captain Edwin Babot dropped his other anchor, but both cables snapped within minutes, so he put on canvas and drove his ship up on the beach, striking about 100 metres north of the *Star*. The crew scrambled ashore with their personal effects.

The last casualty of the evening was unexpected. The *Otago* had got away safely, but at 1730 hours north of the town a murderous wave carried away her rudder. Helpless, Captain Campbell ran her hard aground to save lives. She grounded bow-on, but heavy seas pushed her over. This made escape difficult for the crew, who got ashore with only the clothes they were wearing. The *Otago* broke up quickly, leaving little more than a name board and shattered timbers.

When dawn broke, wool bales and broken timber littered the beaches for kilometres. Not all the wood came from the ships. Much of it came from the town's near-new jetty. The waves had ripped away the outer T-end, and undermined the approaches to it. To make matters worse, most of the Oamaru Landing Service Co and Traill, Roxby & Co surfboats were also ruined. The town was stunned. It was back to square one. But what next?

Chapter Two

'THE BREAKWATER AND NOTHING BUT THE BREAKWATER'
1868–1884

Long before the great storm wrecked their jetty, Oamaruvians had begun to accuse Big Brother Dunedin of neglect. A few inland North Otago farmers churlishly ranked roads and bridges ahead of breakwaters, and it was rumoured that some Oamaru merchants fancied a rail link to Moeraki, but in the town at least the noise and numbers overwhelmingly backed the breakwater. The few 'croakers' were drowned out at public meetings such as the one held at the Northern Hotel in December 1867. There, in the fug of smoke and impassioned debate, the town's merchants swore that using Moeraki would mean delays, double-handling and damage. James Ashcroft called the Moeraki scheme 'a specimen of Bathgate's gas,' a jibe at Dunedin politician John Bathgate. Another Dunedin politico 'had sunk so low as to be found playing the role of a temperance lecturer (loud laughter).'[1] While Ashcroft played to the gallery, the *Oamaru Times* sneered at the superintendent for 'producing a dish whose aroma will doubtless agreeably titillate the noses of the Dunedinites and of those who have a special interest in the spending of the modest sum of £150,000 to make Moeraki the Port Chalmers of Oamaru.'[2] While pledging not to 'raise the cry of "The Breakwater, and nothing but the Breakwater"', the *Times* did precisely that.

Oamaruvians knew they had a fight on their hands. Enemy Number One was the provincial harbourmaster. In happier days Captain William Thomson had commanded coastal steamers but it was now his lot to dish out the province's lamentably inadequate resources to Otago's squabbling ports. There was never enough to go around and Oamaru's chances were lessened because Thomson had developed an abiding dislike for its roadstead during his seagoing days. In his 1866 annual report he put the boot in. Convinced that Otago Harbour would be the only port the province needed once the railways developed, he grudgingly accepted the Oamaru–Moeraki line as a stop-gap: 'sums expended in making Harbors where nature has not already

provided them would be a needless expenditure,' he declared provocatively.[3]

Events played into his hands. In 1868, noting that ten of Otago's twelve wrecks and strandings that year had occurred at Oamaru, he called railways 'the only security against a recurrence of such disasters.'[4] Three years later he dismissed a commission of inquiry's report for a wet dock at Oamaru. If the northern district must have a harbour, Kakanui 'presents far more advantages … than the creek at Oamaru.'[5]

What can we make of this? The reports were wordy and sound odd to modern ears. But if these bewhiskered Victorians' earnest debates seem other-worldly, think of how we squabble over dividing up roading funds. Long before the ugly word 'infrastructure' besmirched our vocabulary, colonials knew that roads, railways and harbours counted. In the 1860s, most put ports first.

But while Dunedin and Oamaru traded insults, petitions and editorials, the anchorage stagnated. Almost the only innovation was the rocket brigade, a unit that used special guns to fire lines to ships in distress. At the heart of the operation was Colonel Edward Boxer's 'Boxer Life-saving Rocket'. When Captain Sewell tested it on 28 August 1869, firing it from opposite Henry France's store to the flagstaff, 300 metres away, the wind carried the rocket left of the target, but distance was more important than pinpoint accuracy, and Sewell was pleased to achieve a distance of 500 metres. Two boatmen on the flagstaff's yard passed the thin line attached to the rocket through the tackle-block, and the ground crew paid out the rope carrying the life-saving basket up to the yard, where one man climbed in and was winched back to the 'supposed shore end'.[6]

In October Mayor Samuel Shrimski led the drive for recruits at the Volunteer Hall. Sewell, who read out the rules of the Tynemouth Life-saving Corps, and explained how brigades worked in Britain, was made leader of the

Oamaru Rocket Brigade.[7] Twenty-two men signed up that night, and many of them were boatmen. They donated their services, but from 1870 the provincial government paid the unit £160 to divide amongst themselves as they saw fit.

The rocket brigade saved lives. The lifeboat did not. This handsome, ten-metre boat arrived in May 1867, another dubious gift from Dunedin's penny-pinching politicians. Within days it failed its first and only test when the schooner *Mary Ann Christina* fired distress rockets above the bay. Volunteers raced to the beach only to discover that that there was no wheeled carriage or ramp to launch the boat safely. In their struggles to drag it seawards, they stove in its bottom, rendering it useless. Fortunately by then the *Mary Ann Christina*'s crew had solved their problems and no longer required assistance. But that was the end of the lifeboat. In 1870 it was said to be 'practically as unavailable for want of proper launching apparatus as if it had been placed on the top of the Horse Range.' Abandoned in the open, it rotted away.[8]

There were few other improvements. The creek north of the landing area was dammed to provide more dry working space for boat crews and the crane near the stump of the jetty was recommissioned, although it was unserviceable for much of 1870–71 after the sea washed away the approach and undermined the track along the base of the Cape. A new signal station was built on the Cape in 1872 but two years later Sewell sought reinstatement of the lower one (removed to provide space for the railway station), since fog or low cloud sometimes obscured the new one.[9]

These minor improvements were no substitute for a breakwater. The question now became one not of whether one would be built – the good Captain Thomson's grumblings aside, few now doubted that – but its size and who would pay. In 1867, the plan had been for a relatively short seawall to protect the jetty. That would have been

North Otago Museum curator Ian Wards holds two launching poles from the rocket brigade. One of the poles carries the inscription 'His Honor the Superintendent'; the other says 'Mr Birt No. 4'. – Gavin McLean

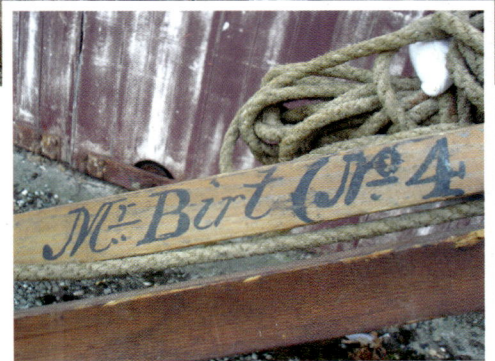

What it was all about. Sixteen ships form the backdrop to this photograph, and a laborious row from the shore. The steamer on the right looks like the Beautiful Star, *a regular on the Dunedin –Oamaru run.* – North Otago Museum 216

Oamaru from Wharfe Street 1874

fine for ships of up to about 300 tons, but not for the London wool ships. They would still play Russian roulette in the roadstead, hamstrung by the slow, costly boating service. Since ship sizes inevitably creep up to offer economies of scale, the more perceptive rejected half-measures. For Oamaru to become a regional powerhouse, it had to match or exceed the facilities offered by its rivals, Port Chalmers and Timaru.

That seemed unlikely, at least in the case of the Otago port. After the February fiasco, the provincial government appointed engineers Edward Dobson and John Blackett – deliberately chosen from outside Otago to quash complaints of bias – to report on options. It asked them three questions: could the Oamaru roadstead be made safe for large seagoing ships; could suitable accommodation be made available for coasters by means of a dock or otherwise; and if neither was possible, could a jetty be built cheaply?

Dobson and Blackett quickly dismissed the deep-sea option, calling 'the shoalness of the water' and 'the defective nature of the holding ground' 'insuperable objections' to accommodating large ships. The best they could suggest was a 100-metre breakwater from the end of the Cape to protect 300-ton ships. It would cost £20,000.

Dobson and Blackett considered accommodating coasters in the bay technically feasible, but uneconomic. A new jetty at the site of the old one – which, by the way, they considered 'judiciously chosen' – would cost £8500. It must be built of iron, high (at least 1.8 metres more than the old one) and undecked to survive heavy seas. A rail-mounted steam crane would take goods to drays at the wharf's shore end. But road access was expensive, because the 1868 storm had badly scoured the old one. A new seawall and road would cost £22,000. Alternatively, a 366-metre-long jetty could be run out from the landing place, but sailing ships would find it harder to approach.

In any case, rolling stock and cranes would make the total bill £33,000.

Instead, Dobson and Blackett backed a local suggestion: a dock, 'with lock gates and training walls through the beach into the deep water, for the purpose of keeping the entrance free from shingle' in the Oamaru lagoon (generally referred to as the Brewery Lagoon). A north training wall would extend to a depth of 2.4 metres at low water spring tide; the curved southern training wall would reach 1.8 metres. The entrance lock would be 48.8 metres long, 7.9 metres wide and the lock sills would be placed 4.1 metres below mean high water mark. Ships drawing 2.7 metres could enter and leave during the last quarter of flood tide and the last quarter of ebb tide. The quoins, aprons, entrance walls and copings would be of Port Chalmers stone, the side walls and inverts of Oamaru stone. Dobson and Blackett costed it at £36,891 for the dock, cranes and four dams in the creek to hold the water for sluicing out any shingle that accumulated at the entrance. The dock 'would enable goods to be landed and discharged in the heart of the town, thus dispensing with both cartage and lighterage.'[10] Unloading cargo in Itchen Street sounded wonderful, though the more thoughtful wondered how long coasters would fit it.

The first half of 1869 was spent preparing plans and wooing politicians. For once, provincial councillors played ball, probably relieved that the dock would forever lock Oamaru into feeder services from Otago Harbour. In November 1868 a public meeting formed a Harbour Works Committee, led by the mayor, politicians and merchants. Dunedin agreed to the formation of the Oamaru Dock Trust.

But then, it was the turn of the engineers to scrap amongst themselves. To the disappointment of locals, Dobson and Blackett refused to oversee the project. George Barr, the provincial chief engineer, prepared drawings, but from Melbourne in September 1869

Dobson sniped that Barr's plans would create 'engineering impossibilities'. 'Even if it could be built … it could not be kept in repair, it could not be safely used by shipping', he sniffed, alleging that Barr's plans would cost £150,000.[11] Then, in December 1869, David Balfour, the Trust's new engineer, drowned off Timaru, causing more delay.

Work finally began in early 1871. On 4 April the *Oamaru Times* reported that day labourers had built three twenty-tonne concrete blocks just east of the old jetty site. Everything was humming along. The men were working on a fourth block and output would increase in a few weeks' time after the arrival of steam machinery and more men were taken on.[12]

Attention now turned to building the seawalls. John McGregor, the trust's new engineer, seems to have worried about shingle building up off the dock entrance. Dobson and Blackett were aware of the problem and had suggested flushing it away by releasing water from dams constructed along the creek. McGregor favoured prevention over cure. Two long seawalls would keep the shingle away from the entrance and create a large sheltered anchorage: one, stretching 425-metres from the Point at the end of the Cape, the other a 150-metre wall north of the dock entrance. The walls would comprise thirty 37-tonne concrete blocks with Oamaru Stone ones sandwiched between. But could Oamaru afford it?

The tenders for McGregor's revised plan far exceeded Dobson and Blackett's £20,000. The Trust was embarrassed, but pressed on. It now called the south-east wall out from the Point the first stage, 'as the success of the inner works would entirely depend on the protection obtained from running out this breakwater.'[13] It would cost £20,000. The *Oamaru Times* agreed that with the walls 'sufficient shelter for shipping will be afforded for years to come, and that the excavation of the dock itself may be for some time postponed.' Although it regretted

not armouring the seaward side with iron, it considered the trial concrete blocks tough enough to withstand the sea's fury.

Press on, press on, was the town's attitude.

The change from a minor dock to a deep-sea port unsettled Dunedin's politicians. First, they forced the trustees to tender the inner works (£40,000). Then they quibbled over the schedule for payments. At one stage Provincial Superintendent James Macandrew asked the trustees to consider making cement from Moeraki boulders![14] He also declined to supply Maori war prisoners as labourers. But McGregor and North Otago politicians lobbied effectively, and on 4 May the Trust gained permission to 'substitute the outer wall for the part now being commenced by the contractors [Walkem & Peyman].' The dock was effectively dead. By June, workers had blasted rock from around the jetty stump to create a working area for block construction, and the Trust had accepted a £3100 contract to build a tramway to the Point. Oamaru papers were running advertisements 'Wanted, 30 Good PICK and SHOVEL MEN. Constant work. Apply Oamaru breakwater.'

Walkem & Peyman started well, but by September they were being delayed by the government's slow payments.[15] It was just the first of a painful series of glitches and delays. At times things went smoothly. In October 1873 the *North Otago Times* reported that eight blocks had been laid the previous week. By mid November the wall had reached 67 metres from the shore and the centre portion had been raised high enough to operate the travelling crane safely. But in November congestion in the block-making area slowed work, and workers had to be diverted to reclaiming more land. By Christmas the foundation blocks for another pocket had been laid and, given fine weather, it was expected to lengthen the wall by 4.25 metres that week. A 200-tonne capacity cement store was also nearing completion.

Start of Breakwater. Oamaru. 1872.

The biggest travelling crane in the world, the second biggest or the biggest south of the line? Claims made on behalf of the 'Moa' varied, but the machine (photographed later than the 1872 date inscribed on the print) was undoubtedly massive for the day. In a sense, Oamaru's hopes were riding on it. Thomas Forrester, the town's renowned architect, and the harbour board's secretary and engineer, is on the footplate, at the left.
— *North Otago Museum 1900*

The contractors learned as they went along. They built the first section (about 240 metres) of two rows of concrete blocks flanking a rubble-filled cavity. Beyond that point, as wave action grew stronger, they reverted to solid concrete construction. On a short base, four tiers of blocks were placed, each 3.66 metres wide. The blocks were tied together by a larger block, called a monolith, 3.66 metres wide on the top tier, but raised and 6.28 metres wide at the top; this effectively cemented the top row of blocks together. Then a problem emerged. The composition of the seabed varied considerably; in the softer places, blocks moved with wave action. About 300 metres out, therefore, the contractors sat the wider monolith atop the tiers and added an apron block at the bottom of the seaward side to armour it.[16]

Picks and shovels had their place, but only steam power could place the massive concrete blocks. So Walkem & Peyman ordered a massive travelling crane from Kincaid and McQueen, which built it at its Cumberland Street premises in Dunedin. It reached Oamaru early in

Contrasting moods. The technical challenges were less daunting than the weather. The waves got rougher as the breakwater pushed further out into the bay, sometimes slowing work for weeks on end. It must have been appallingly wet and cold in winter, but the unemployment and poverty caused by the Long Depression from the late 1870s meant that workmen always looked forward to every extension of the contract. The crane used the wide rail tracks and the blocks were wheeled out along the narrower tramline. – *North Otago Museum 4049 and 4058*

LESS THAN IMPRESSED

The Dunedin steamers were better than a slow, bumpy coach service from Dunedin, but they were far from perfect, especially before the completion of Macandrew Wharf freed passengers from the inconvenience of having to use the surfboats. In June 1873 the *Otago Witness*'s correspondent wondered if prosperity had made the boating crews complacent:

Things generally in this district are particularly lively at present. One is very forcibly reminded of this on entering Oamaru bay or roadstead, where some seven or eight vessels, some of them of large tonnage, are tremulously anchored. The Boating Companies' men are worked off their legs, and yet are not able to overtake the work. The Samson had to return to Dunedin the other day without any cargo; not but what there was plenty for her, but it could not be boated off for lack of boats and men. The Maori on Sunday night called in by appointment to land some passengers, but the men struck and would not go off to her, though it was a beautiful calm moonlight night, and so she had to remain anchored in the bay till the morning, thereby losing a whole day in her passage to Timaru and Lyttelton. There is a fine opportunity at present for an enterprising man of nautical experience to start another Boating Company in Oamaru.[17]

A year later, Joseph Jones wrote to the editor of the *North Otago Times* a tongue-in-cheek complaint about the service offered by the *Samson*:

Sir, — As a passenger by the Samson lately, I should like to complain a little — not that any benefit will result, but it will amuse me and relieve my mind. As usual, she was advertised to start at 10 a.m., but the agents, knowing the fallibility of human nature, added a margin of half-an-hour, and announced to all and sundry inquiring that the boat would leave the beach at halfpast 10, and that there was no possibility of doubt whatever but that 11 o'clock would find us fairly on our way to Dunedin. It is a good and beneficial thing to have time for meditation and self examination, and some such benevolent idea apparently actuated Messrs Aitken and Co., who accordingly, with kind consideration, managed affairs so that fully two hours were placed at the disposal of those inclined for this or any other light and elegant recreation on the Oamaru beach, not to mention the easy chairs placed conveniently for any tired of standing, and the refreshments handed round free gratis, and for nothing, so that our last thoughts of Oamaru should be pleasant ones. Yet, this is my complaint that the ungrateful passengers weren't satisfied, but grumbled, forsooth, merely because they did not start until three hours past the advertised time, and several of them told me that they very rarely got away by steamer except in that erratic sort of manner, and one of my informants believed that it was an ingenious device of those having the ordering of things Samsonial, to teach men not to put trust in Princes or Steamboat Agents.

Now, Sir, you are naturally a good man, please write a leader on the subject of ingratitude, because, though this letter is only written on account of one particular trip, yet everybody says that the same kind forethought and tender care on the part of our Samson friends is the rule, not the exception. For my part I shall be happy to contribute my mite towards the erection of a suitable sarcophagus for the captain and agents — immediate possession to be taken.[20]

August 1873, 'in the presence of "ladies fair and many townsmen".[18] The *Evening Star* printed this description:

> The platform is composed of eight iron girders, each about twenty feet in length, riveted together in the form of a gridiron. It is mounted on twelve wheels, with double flanges, and will travel on two sets of rails of about three feet gauge. On the platform a framework of iron of similar design, but not so massive, is placed, and on this the crane engine and driving machinery are mounted. The crane itself differs little as regards design from other cranes, but its ponderous proportions exceed those of any similar machine manufactured in New Zealand. The mast is a solid casting, three tons weight, and about nine feet in length, and the tubular jibs weigh each about a ton. The perpendicular frames weigh each about a ton. The engine is a pretty thing of seven-horse power nominal, and the machine altogether, when completed, will weigh between thirty-five and forty tons. It has a lifting capacity of forty tons, and when laden and ballasted will weigh altogether about 120 tons.[19]

That its construction was a remarkable feat for a young colonial engineering works was undeniable. But how big was it? Newspapers liked to call it the world's second-largest, bested only by one at Madras, India; sometimes it was the world's biggest. What can be said with certainty is that at a time when a two- or three-tonne lift was average for a large steam crane, 'Moa', Oamaru's machine, was enormous. On 23 August 1873 the *Waikato Times* reported that it had lifted 30 tonnes successfully.

Today it is hard to understand the pride people took in such huge slabs of concrete. But the Oamaruvians of 1875 had no doubt. They treasured the safety and certainty brought by being able to step on and off a steamer moored snugly behind the breakwater. On 6 May, the day the governor officially opened Macandrew Wharf, the *North Otago Times* crowed that the schooner *Elderslie* had berthed 'as snug and secure alongside the wharf at Oamaru as she could be at the pier at Port Chalmers'. Surely this was 'convincing proof that the Oamaru Breakwater is a success?'[21] So good was the wharf that in December 1875 the board gave the Oamaru–Dunedin ferry steamer priority over other shipping; in May 1876 the skipper of the steamer *Matau* flouted this rule, and moved only after a hastily-convened harbour board meeting resolved not to supply cargo to him.

Architect David Ross's austere wooden immigrants' barracks overlook the Esplanade signal station and the railway station. Surf boats are still tucked in under the bank below the barrack fence. After a few years the building was turned over to the local benevolent society. – North Otago Museum 2539

A few 'croakers' lobbed insults at the breakwater – in 1877 'Crustacean' doubted that 'this juvenile excrescence is going to run Dunedin for its bare life' – but most people trumpeted its advance as another landmark in Oamaru's 'career of prosperity and progress.' Local papers compared it favourably with similar works in Britain and championed the modern engineering principles behind its design.[22]

As more ships used the wharf, the demand for the landing service diminished. Once there were two rival companies – in November 1873 the newspaper reported their boats out in the bay awaiting the steamer *Taiaroa* ('there being a smart race between the two boats' crews as to who should reach the steamer first') – but by the time the harbour board took over in 1875, there was just one, its boats used only to work the ships too big to come inside the breakwater.

Macandrew Wharf's completion also virtually eliminated the need for the rocket brigade. The Oamaru Harbour Board (which replaced the dock trust in 1874) saw less reason to fund it as facilities developed. In January 1881 board member Samuel Shrimski asked what their £24 bought: 'the brigade never turned out and in fact was a dead letter.' The secretary replied that the reduced sum merely funded a nucleus crew; in an emergency, volunteers would be needed. The board paid the money grudgingly on condition the brigade drilled at least six-monthly. In 1881, at Captain Sewell's suggestion, all harbour board staff were enrolled in the brigade, and the board's payment was converted to an accident fund.[23] By April 1883 the brigade must have been dead, because the paper was reporting rumours of an attempt to 'resuscitate' it. Four years later the board transferred the rocket equipment to the Oamaru Navals, who used it in exercises and on holidays such as Queens Birthday.

People remained as important as cargo, none more so than immigrants. In the early 1870s colonial treasurer Julius Vogel launched an ambitious works programme and immigration drive. Vogel knew that more people would expand the market for industries and pay for roads, bridges, railways and ports. Every centre wanted its share of migrants. The big clippers carrying them generally called at the main ports, and Oamaruvians often grumbled that Dunedin took the best and gave it the leftovers. They may have been right about a group that arrived at the wharf fighting-drunk: 'some damage was done to the barrack-master and other officials before they could be herded to their quarters.'[24] In 1874, at the peak of the Vogel wave, the government built a large wooden barracks above the landing area on the site of the old government store. Dunedin architect David Ross designed a two-storey building, 36.27 metres long and 7 metres wide. It was divided into separate spaces for married couples (12 rooms) and single males (two spaces, one holding 20 beds, the other 21) and single females (one open room with beds for 21 single women and children) It could accommodate 86 adults and 'a number of children'.[25] The interior was lined with dressed wood, tongued and grooved. The barracks master was Alfred Hesketh, who was also the town's immigration officer. In 1874 sixteen cottages in four blocks were built on the hill above it.[26]

Initially, Oamaru's quota of immigrants landed at Port Chalmers and came up by the steamers *Maori* or *Waitaki*. From 1879 they came by rail. As always, the old guard scrutinised the newcomers closely. On 26 January 1879 the *Waitaki* brought up a batch from the ship *Taranaki*. 'They will be open for engagement to-day, with the exception of the single girls, for whom application should be made tomorrow', the paper reported. Next day it complained about one man who 'commenced by misbehaving himself on the Normanby Wharf and subsequently endeavoured to amuse himself by kicking Mr Hesketh [the Dunedin immigration agent] and resisting the police in the execution of their duty.'[27] He was fined £5 and reinforced suspicions that Dunedin grabbed the best and sent the riff-raff to Oamaru.

On 6 May 1875 the Marquis of Normanby opened
Macandrew Wharf. The 120 guests who crammed into three
carriages and open trucks for the short trip to the breakwater
were Oamaru's first rail passengers. At the wharf, Lady
Normanby told the diver there was no need to submerge for
her, but Their Excellencies closely inspected the concrete blocks
and the steam crane: 'one of the most powerful, if not the most
powerful, in the world.' After 'throwing a bottle of champagne
a little distance from him', the governor christened Macandrew
Wharf in honour of superintendent James Macandrew, who
windily predicted that Oamaru would become one of the most
important ports in the colony: 'bye and bye, they might see …
docks rivalling the London Docks.' – North Otago Museum 4192

Three years later, as a sideline to opening the main trunk
railway, Lord Normanby opened a bigger wharf named after
him. At George Sumpter's new grain store afterwards he
put on the Victorian equivalent of fast food – the joints being
pre-carved to enable them eat in just twenty minutes. Even so,
they toasted 'The Queen', 'the Prince of Wales and the Royal
Family', 'His Excellency the Governor', 'Success and Prosperity
to Oamaru!', and 'the Ministry and Members of Parliament'.
The steamer Waitaki is at Macandrew Wharf.
– North Otago Museum 4192

The breakwater proved its worth even incomplete. In this photograph, taken about 1875–76, steam cranes are unloading a steamer at Macandrew Wharf, while two small sailing vessels shelter in its lee. To modern eyes, Oamaru seems rather distant, showing how the reclamations later reduced the size of the bay. – *North Otago Museum 4035*

A few years later, around 1879–80: The breakwater has advanced further and ships occupy Macandrew, Normanby and the Cross wharves. – *North Otago Museum 4039*

The view from the other side. Timber is stacked alongside the tramway which hugs the shoreline out to the cramped breakwater construction site, explaining why for decades the Railways Department officially termed this branch 'Oamaru Breakwater'. The big steam crane 'Moa' is near the tip of the partly-built breakwater. At Macandrew Wharf smaller steam cranes are unloading a brigantine and two surf boats which have probably brought cargo from the ship moored in the outer anchorage; three sailing vessels are tucked in under the lee of the breakwater. – Ian Farquhar

'FROM OAMARU TO DUNEDIN … IN FOUR HOURS' – THE *WAITAKI*

The Dunedin steamers, the Wallace *and* Geelong *in the 1860s, and the* Samson, Maori *and* Beautiful Star *in the 1870s, were Oamaruvians' lifeline to the world.*

In 1875 local merchants got together with the Union Steam Ship Company to build a ship especially for the run. The Oamaru and Dunedin Steam Ship Company ordered a 412-ton (228 tons register) screw steamer from Wingate & Co of Glasgow. The *Waitaki* was 50.3 metres long and 6.7 metres in width and cruised at 12 knots, burning eight to ten tonnes of coal a day. She left Glasgow on 7 July 1876, and reached Dunedin on 3 October.

The *North Otago Times*'s Port Chalmers correspondent thought her ugly: 'She is not a taking vessel to the eye, her appearance being heavy in consequence of her lines and a heavy stringer on each side. She is plumb stemmed and narrow for her length, and thus her deck space is somewhat cramped.' But below decks was different: the saloon accommodation was 'very superior'. A wide staircase leading to it was teak-panelled in the sides with maple half-round pilasters between, and surmounted by gilt cornice and architraves. The saloon ('a noble apartment') was 32 feet long; around its sides were locker-settees, faced with horsehair cushions and covered with crimson velvet. 'The backs lift up to form sleeping berths, and sleeping places can also be improvised on the transom, and on a wide ledge between the backs of the settees and the sides of the steamer.' Forty beds could be made up here. In the centre of the saloon was a long oak table, and around it velvet-covered seats. The paper said much less about the steerage accommodation, under the main deck, which also included ladies' cabins.

The *Waitaki* left Port Chalmers at 0830 hours on Friday 13 October, carrying 25 passengers and 90 tonnes of cargo, commanded by the *Samson*'s popular Captain Edie. A fresh southerly was blowing and the ship berthed at the breakwater on time at 1300 hours. 'A large number of citizens were on the wharf when the *Waitaki* came alongside and directly she was moored they rushed aboard and began exploring the vessel from stem to stern.' An hour later, with 400–500 aboard, the ship left the breakwater and cruised out to Boundary Creek. The heavy swell had many leaning over the rail, 'one going so far as to make his hat an offering to the deep', but most were highly impressed by the time the *Waitaki* docked at Macandrew Wharf at 1500 hours.

Half an hour later, 40 men, mostly merchants, were in the saloon, tucking into 'every delicacy that money could procure'. After eating and drinking heartily, they went through a series of wordy toasts and speeches. The company, the captain, the harbour board, the harbour master, the railways, the merchants, even the ship's steward and 'the Ladies' were invoked as excuses to raise another glass. In proposing a toast to Union Company managing director James Mills, Dr Garland predicted that 'when travellers could proceed from Oamaru to Dunedin in the *Waitaki* in four hours he felt sure that for the future passengers travelling by coach would be few and far between.'

Sandwiched between these speeches and toasts were 'musical numbers'. They sound a mixed bag. F. Humphries offered 'The Elephant Walks Around'; G. R. Taylor, 'A Life on the Ocean Wave'; T. Fairlie, 'Remember Me'; F. Humphries, 'I run 'em in'; R.L. Rule. 'Tis But a Little Faded Flower'; Mr Christie, 'Scots Wha Hae' and David Millar gave 'an amusing Scotch recitation'. 'Three cheers were then given for the chairman and vice-chairman, and "Auld Lang Syne" and a verse of the National Anthem having been sung, the company disembarked, a special train conveying them to the railway station, arriving in town about 7 o'clock.'

The *Waitaki* had two good years, running alongside the *Samson*, but the completion of the main trunk rail line in September 1878 ate into her trade. The *Samson* was withdrawn, and the *Waitaki* ran three times a week, sailing at night except on Sundays. The company slashed fares, but sailings dropped to two a week in April 1879 and the ship was withdrawn in August. Smaller, older ships, the *Beautiful Star* and the *Maori*, maintained an Oamaru–Dunedin service until 1890 – but nothing recaptured the magic of the *Waitaki*'s glory days.[28]

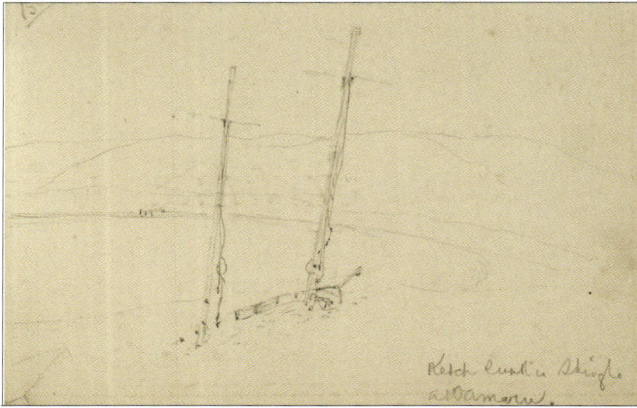

The ketch Franklin Belle *was the cargo carrier wrecked at Oamaru. She arrived in port on 20 June 1879 heavily laden with iron rails, and moored off Normanby Wharf. There her anchor started to drag. The crew of the* Good Templar *offered help, but before they could lift the anchors, heavy seas smashed her hatches and flooded her hold. Captain Henry Matheson beached her at the mouth of the lagoon, where she struck old concrete blocks lying on the beach and stuck fast in the shingle. Salvors tried to extract her in November but gave up within days. Arthur Haylock's pencil sketch shows her still buried there a year later. – Alexander Turnbull Library E-060-3-001*

The berthage situation was greatly improved in 1878–79, by which time Oamaru had 370 metres of sheltered wharf space. Friday 6 September 1878 was one of the great days in Oamaru's history. The governor, Lord Normanby, arrived by train accompanied by politicians and officials. The highlight was the official opening of the latest section of the South Island main trunk, giving Oamaru rail access to Dunedin. But there was another ceremony, the naming of the port's newest and largest wharf, so the vice-regal party took a train to the breakwater where the flagstaff and the ships were flying bunting. At harbour board chairman George Sumpter's suggestion, Lord Normanby christened the concrete wharf 'Normanby Wharf' with champagne. Then they returned to the town, where Sumpter's new grain store had seating for 350, the caterer having carved the meat and poultry 'so that no time was thrown away in that direction, the party proceeding to the pleasant task of mastication.'[29]

No. 3 Wharf, which ran parallel to the Cape and covered two thirds of the distance between Normanby Wharf and the breakwater, was finished a few months later. In February 1879 the *North Otago Times* reported that it had been completed by Miller and Smillie and was waiting only for the Railways to connect the tracks for ships to use it. The wharf, simply called the Cross Wharf, opened without ceremony, but with its completion 'the

unsightly "tip" at the seaward side of the bridge has been entirely removed to fill up No. 3 Wharf.' In January 1879 workmen also finished widening Macandrew Wharf's inner berth by about a metre to bring it into line with the outer berth, making movement easier for the steam cranes. With the completion of this extra wharf space, the contractors laid off their labourers and the harbour board its boatmen. It also brought a new problem: ships crowding in behind the breakwater and sometimes even entering the inner anchorage against the harbourmaster's instructions.

The final layout of the port was fixed in 1880, when the board voted to enclose the basin with a rubble mole running out from the end of Wansbeck Street. Captain Sewell had insisted on its construction to reduce the effects of surge on ships moored at the Cross Wharf and the eastern berth at Normanby Wharf. But setting the starting point divided the board. In early 1881 they conducted a brief, but crucial, debate on the size of the port. James Hassell and Henry Aitken led the financial conservatives. Hassell tried to start the mole half-way between Arun Street and Wansbeck Street, reducing the harbour area and shortening the breakwater by sixty metres. He was motivated by 'a strict determination not to borrow another six-pence' and the fear that farmers would rail their produce to Timaru if Oamaru's port fees went up. He was certain that 'forty-five acres would be quite sufficient for fifty years.' Others disagreed. After some uncertainty and delay, the board backed the Wansbeck Street alignment (disappointing the few who favoured Itchen Street). Three years later, fresh concerns about debt focussed discussion on the mole. After heated debate, Aitken had it stopped slightly short and replaced the planned concrete end with sloped rocks.[30]

Rock started coming out of the breakwater quarry long before the board confirmed its 1881 decision. It was not very durable, and the volume of waste and rock debris

'CAPTAIN'S LOG' – THE *SWORDFISH*, 1882

What was it like to visit Oamaru in the age of sail?
The log of the Australian schooner Swordfish *is a very rare survival from the*
age of sail. The 156-ton schooner brought a cargo of Hobart timber.
I have kept Captain Delmer's eccentric spelling,
but have added punctuation.

Thursday 19 January

7 a.m. sighted Oamaru town. Steering for it. 8.30 outside the breakwater. Come to an anchor. Hault in & moored here at the buoys, this being our berths.
[Delmer was unlucky with his timing. The port, which had only Macandrew, Normanby and Cross Wharfs, was crowded. The *North Otago Times* of 20 January reported that there was a record tonnage of shipping (2134 tons) inside the breakwater: barques *Mountaineer*, *Gwendoline* and *Examiner*; barquentines *Louise* and *Frey*; brigantine *Peerless*, and the schooner *Swordfish*. George Sumpter was the ship's agent, and after the initial report, the *Times* referred to the *Swordfish* as a brigantine.]

Friday 20 January

6 a.m. Hault alongside the wharf & started discharging. Worked till 5 p.m. Had to haul off to the moorings. Light winds with thick weather throughout the day.

Saturday 21 January

6 a.m. Light southerly wind with thick rainy weather. Received order from the harbour Department to heave out to the anchor[age?] on account of them letting of[f] a heavy blast on the bank. Midnight very heavy surge carrying away the stern warp almost as fast as we put them out. Bar[ometer] 28.60 Very little winds. Took all our time to run out warps and attend to the ship.
[The blast Delmer referred to was fired in the cliff opposite Normanby Wharf a little after 8 p.m. The paper reported surprisingly little noise and no scattered rocks, but the charge did bring down 12,000 yards of rock and spoil.]

Sunday 22 January

8 a.m. received a big hawser from the shore & run out on the port quarter to the mooring buoy. Winds strong WNW. Took all our time to attend to the ship. Noon, Bar 29.10 Wind fresh SE

Monday 23 January

6 a.m. hault alongside of the wharf & started discharging. Worked til 5 p.m. Light N.E. winds with fine clear weather throughout the day, Bar 29.40

Tuesday 24 January

6 a.m. made to haul ahead to make room for a steamer [the Beautiful Star] going into the wharf & then put out 7 truck loads of timber, then delaid for the want of trucks. 5 p.m. hault out to the mooring – steamer to occupy the wharf tomorrow. Light winds from NE through the day. Bar 29.41

[The steamer at the berth on Wednesday was the Dunedin-Oamaru ferry *Maori*.]

Wednesday 25 January

At 4 p.m. hove in and moored alongside the wharf. Crew employed various throughout the day. Wind Easterly with fine weather through the day. Bar 29.19

Thursday 26 January

Started work at 8.30 a.m. and worked till 5 p.m. Fresh N.E. wind through the day with clear weather. Bar 29.15

Friday 27 January

Started discharging at 8.30 finished unloading by 11.00 a.m. Noon began taking in ballast. 5 p.m. got all the ballast on board, 50 tons, vessel drawing 8 feet 4 inches [2.5 metres] aft and 7 feet 7 inches [2.3 metres] forward. Hault out from the wharf & moored to the mooring buoys fore and aft. Winds strong west through the day with clear weather. Bar 20.10

Saturday/Sunday 28/29 January

Cleaned up on the deck and placed the long boat ready for sea, painted her round on the starboard side. Wind West, a gale through the day. Bar 29.10. Variable winds.
Variable winds with fine clear weather. Bat 29.35

Monday 30 January

Strong northerly winds with clear weather throughout the day. Bar 29.35 Crew employed variously about the rigging & painting outside.

Tuesday 31 January

Fresh breezes from North to N.W. Bar 29.08 Crew repairing the mainsail & various jobs about the rigging.

Wednesday 1 February

This 24 [hours] have commenced with Strong S.W. Winds & heavy rain. 6 a.m. Harbour Master came on board, unmoored & made sail 7 a.m. past out clear of the Breakwater with winds South fresh with thick rainy weather. Noon less wind. 4 p.m. calm & light variable winds. Bar 29.38 All sails sett.[31]

[The *North Otago Times* was at variance with the log, reporting the *Swordfish* as having sailed from Oamaru on the 30th for Australia via the Kaipara.]

'THE SIMPLEST LIGHTHOUSE ON OUR COAST OR PERHAPS ANY OTHER'

'At Oamaru is to be found the simplest lighthouse on our coast or perhaps any other', 'Fabian Bell' wrote in the Otago Witness *in 1902, in his survey of New Zealand's lighthouses. 'It is but a cottage with a little bay window on the eastern side, in which a light is shown to indicate the position of the harbour.'*

Captain Thomson's stub of a snub. The Cape Wanbrow lighthouse was a simple calioptric kerosene light in the front window of the keeper's cottage. In 1873 the provincial harbourmaster, no admirer of Oamaru, ruled that 'the efficiency of lights does not depend on the ornamental buildings and machinery at present in use – the cost of which very much interferes with the illumination of our coast at all prominent points.' Oamaruvians disagreed, but failed to have their light upgraded from a harbour light to a coastal light.
– North Otago Museum 2796

Cute and vernacular were not qualities Victorian Oamaruvians prized. In those days the colonial government was responsible for the main lights, the coastal lights. The provincial governments and harbour boards looked after the harbour lights. Oamaru merchants wanted a light, preferably one of the former; 123 of them petitioned the government for a coastal light. James Balfour had thought Oamaru needed a decent light, but he was dead and Marine Department Nautical Advisor Captain Robert Johnson opposed such thinking. The seabed off Cape Wanbrow was comparatively regular and the adjacent coast quite safe, so he preferred to spend the government's money at Moeraki, where the notorious Fish Reef imperiled coasters making for Oamaru and Timaru. Building at Oamaru would be: 'an utter waste of public money; and were no settlement in existence at Oamaru, the idea of placing a light there never would have suggested itself to the mind of any practical man.'[32]

On 22 April the Moeraki light, an 8.3-metre white-painted wooden tower housing a '3rd-order dioptric white light' was illuminated for the first time. The light was visible for up to nineteen nautical miles. On the same night the fixed white light on Cape Wanbrow was altered to red and the fixed red light on the end of the breakwater was changed to green. But it was near-invisible in fog, and even a fifth-order red light failed to overcome that problem. The harassed harbour board tried and failed to hand the light to the Marine Department, so in the early 1890s upgraded the light to a catadioptric lantern, lighting the sea for a distance of 15 nautical miles.[33]

The automated replacement built during World War II was even less imposing. In fact, coastal skippers used a better, albeit highly informal navigation beacon, the massive neon boot that towered over the Thames Street premises of McDiarmid's shoe shop. Neither survives; the shell of the Cape Wanbrow lighthouse, photographed here in 2006, was disestablished in 1995.
– Gavin McLean

delayed progress, but it had the merit – overwhelming in the board's eyes – of being cheap and close to hand. The quarry blasts were the greatest show in town. In numbers that would horrify modern site safety officials, Victorian Oamaruvians flocked to the waterfront for each blast. On the evening of Saturday 16 January 1881, for example, nearly 1000 people – almost a quarter of the town – turned out to watch half a tonne of gunpowder go off at the end of a tunnel driven into the rock. Three minutes after the contractor lit the fuse, 'the upheaval was great, and cast forth a dense volume of black smoke and pieces of rock.' Smoke was fine, but rock was not. Sewell had cleared shipping away from the danger zone and the railway track had been covered with timber to protect it.

Nevertheless, rocks rained down on the *William and Jane* and boulders shot past the end of the breakwater. There, many 'adventurous persons' who had gone out on to the breakwater 'hazarded their lives'; rocks soared over their heads, although 'their nerves received such a shock by the explosion that they are not so likely to so rashly expose themselves to danger again.' One man was hit in the head by a splinter, after a boulder smashed into a wooden post.[34]

The completion of the stone wharves brought a new problem: shoaling. Sand and shingle swept in behind the breakwater accumulated against the seaward end and against Macandrew Wharf, causing problems there. In 1879, therefore, the board debated buying a dredge.

Sink big. The workers in the boats have an air of expectancy, justifiably. because the odd wooden structure in the background is one four wooden caissons that were ballasted, towed to the end of the breakwater, sunk and then filled with 600–700 tonnes of concrete to form the 'impregnable head to the breakwater'; another caisson is being built on land behind the Cross Wharf .The photograph was probably taken between January and March 1883 when the large caissons were sunk; bad weather delayed the fourth, smaller one. – North Otago Museum 4050

Previously everyone had assumed that the seabed was too rocky to dredge economically. That year, however, Thomas Forrester supervised trial bores that dispelled this myth. In June he reported that three borings made off the end of the breakwater revealed that 'the surface consists of a layer of sand, from one to two feet in thickness, which being removed exposes the hard surface of a shingly conglomerate forming the bottom', hard to pierce but once broken easy to dredge 'to any required depth, and, so far as I can see, without the use of explosive compounds.'[35] It was a revelation, a turning point in the history of town and port. Now it was possible to bring the biggest ships inside the breakwater and do away with open sea lightering.

What sort of dredge was needed? Eventually, and after great debate and dithering, the board awarded a contract to Davidson and Conyers of Dunedin to build a 244-ton bucket dredge from components supplied by a British firm. Unfortunately, the contractors went into receivership and the contract was transferred to Briscoe & Co. The ship was launched at Port Chalmers on 11 February 1883 about a year behind schedule. She steamed up to Oamaru on 30 May and was christened *Progress* – that magical Victorian word! – by George Sumpter's daughter Beatrice next day. She set to work dredging out the berths and swinging area for a new export wharf to serve the frozen meat trade.

The year 1884 was the 'annus mirabilis' for the Port of Oamaru. While it was true that, as historian K.C. McDonald observed, in 1878 (the year the main trunk line connected Oamaru to Christchurch and Dunedin) the town 'was turning its back on the ocean' and that the harbour 'was no longer the dominant feature of the town,' cargo volumes kept climbing and ships got bigger. The data collection by the railways has probably obscured the continued growth of coastal shipping. Many small ships and ports were ousted by the iron horse, but trains also created business for ships through their appetite for coal. As well, the new steamers were very much bigger than their predecessors. Historian Rollo Arnold estimated

that if the tonne-mileages are calculated for 1885, coastal shipping did 7–14 times the business of rail.[36] In fact, Oamaruvians still took steamers from their town, and most would have still considered that the harbour's expansion was crucial to their prosperity.[37]

The year started positively on 1 February, when Miller successfully laid the last monolith at the end of the breakwater, just a year behind schedule. Back in December 1882, the launching of the first of the four large caissons which would form the head of the breakwater had been reported. These big wooden boxes, 7.62 metres long and deep and 5.18 metres wide, were floated out to the end of the breakwater, filled with cement and bound together with a concrete cap to 'constitute an impregnable head to the breakwater'.[38] The contractors had to dredge and flatten the seabed prior to sinking the caissons, which they expected to begin in January 1883. But they needed flat calm conditions to align and sink them, and 1883 was a stormy year. Delay followed delay, but by February 1884 they had placed the last big block. Now all they needed to

The progress industry. They did humble, unglamorous work, scooping muck off the seabed, but colonial Victorians saw dredges as engines of progress and named them appropriately: Otago's was New Era *and Oamaru's was the* Progress, *no less. Seen here clanking away off the mole, she kept twelve men in work: dredge master, sailing master, engineer, two firemen, two winch hands, three deckhands, cook and a night watchman.* – North Otago Museum 2913

do was to repair some storm-damaged blocks and erect a short tower at the end for a small navigation light.

In January 1884, the *Progress* returned from an expensive overhaul at Port Chalmers. So far she had struggled to penetrate the seabed, which was tougher than expected. She had also taken longer than expected to discharge the clay, which was unusually sticky. She was taking two to three hours to fill her hopper and three to four to empty it, limiting her to a load a day. So McGregor and Forrester modified her winches and gearings to break the seabed crust better and fitted chains to the hopper to make discharging faster. These improvements enabled her to dump two loads a day.

Just in time. Local pastoralist John Reid had come up with a plan to bring a new class of ship to Oamaru. In March 1883 he had visited Britain, primed by harbour board members and merchants to market the port. 'Our desire was to get the rates of insurance to our port reduced, and also to satisfy shipowners that our harbour was perfectly safe for vessels drawing 18 to 20 feet of water', he later recalled.[39]

Reid carried photographs and all the statistics the board could provide, but they were less useful than striking up a friendship with a Glasgow ship owner on the voyage to Britain. T.C.C. Guthrie had visited Oamaru and thought it had a great future. He opened many doors for Reid. Even so, the pastoralist had his work cut

out. Some ship owners doubted they could earn enough to pay for insulating a steamer for such a long voyage. Several, including the New Zealand Shipping Co, turned him down or demanded prohibitive guarantees. Reid eventually struck a deal to bring the *Delhi* to Oamaru to load for London, but that fell through, and after some nervous, uncertain weeks, he raised his sights: a large ship built specially to trade between London and Oamaru, to be named *Elderslie* after his estate.[40] Since sailing ships still dominated the UK trade, the *Elderslie* would 'make quite a revolution in the business of the port.'[41] The shipowners, the Scottish firm of Turnbull, Martin & Co, were keen to break into the New Zealand trade. The 2761-ton *Elderslie* was the ancestor of the Scottish Shire Line.

But was the port ready? The news that the *Elderslie* and Shaw Savill & Albion's freezer ship *Dunedin* were expected at Oamaru in August to load for London put new pressure on the board. Fortunately, they had fixed the *Progress* in the nick of time. Her previous inability to deepen the

Reefer gladness. The frozen meat steamer Elderslie *lies alongside Sumpter Wharf as the* Progress *battles sand and silt. Like most first-generation Home boats, the* Elderslie *also carried auxiliary sails, though they were seldom used.*
— Dominion Museum

harbour near the new No. 4 Wharf (Sumpter Wharf) had been responsible for the delay in work beginning after the Timaru firm Philp & Jones signed the contract in August 1883. The site was on the southern edge of the harbour, west of Normanby Wharf, and Thomas Forrester aligned the wharf towards the harbour entrance to minimise the effect of surge.

The refurbished *Progress* worked with new determination. By March 1884 she had deepened the water either side of the wharf to about 7.3 metres at low water and Macandrew Wharf's outer berth to 5.5 metres. The contractors made quick work of the ironbark wharf. By late March, they had almost completed the 70-metre curved viaduct that ran out over volcanic rock and had driven two-thirds of the piers for the 90-metre main section of the wharf. On 5 July 1884, the *North Otago Times* reported that the *Dunedin* would be towed to Oamaru next day and berthed at Sumpter Wharf next morning. It was a race against time: 'The approaches will be finished early this afternoon and the work of laying the rails is being carried out expeditiously and will be ready for the engine this evening.'

The tug *Koputai* brought the *Dunedin* alongside at 1000 hours on Monday 7 July. 'From the Esplanade a large number of persons beheld her arrival and on the wharf were assembled a number of our chief citizens including several ladies.' A boy fell between ship and wharf, but escaped with only a ducking. It was a time to celebrate. A rumour that Port Chalmers' interests had offered to pay to rail North Otago meat there for export was circulating,

and an Oamaru paper rejoiced that 'such knavish tricks were frustrated. From today a new and brighter era has commenced in this port and in this town.'[42]

It was indeed a busy, happy time for the port, with Totara Estate sending 350 sheep carcasses a day to the *Dunedin* for freezing. On 19 July the press reported a record tonnage in port: the ship *Dunedin*, loading meat at Sumpter Wharf for London; the barque *Claribel* just finished loading for Auckland; the brig *Chieftain*, loading produce at Normanby Wharf for Auckland; the barquentine *May*, loading at the Cross Wharf for Adelaide; the barque *Rose M.* at Macandrew Wharf, discharging Newcastle coal; the barque *Mercia*, awaiting a berth to discharge; and the steamer *Beautiful Star* at Macandrew Wharf. Shipping totalling 3461 tons register lay in port.

The *Progress* towed the *Dunedin* out of port on 17 August. She had finished loading a week earlier, but low depths on the West Coast bar entrances had delayed delivery of the coal for her freezing chamber. In her time in port, Captain Whitson and his crew had made friends. The merchants gave him an inscribed gold locket and chain, and the men got to know the locals, some perhaps too well. Several were charged with desertion. 'Deserted, Your Worship; why, you couldn't drive me from her. I only came to town to pay Mrs Grant eighteen pence I owed her, and to get another drink,' he told the judge. 'You wouldn't want me to leave without paying my debts, and give the ship a bad name, would you?' No feelings were hurt, for as she cleared Sumpter Wharf, another seaman charged with desertion cried out 'Three cheers for the bobbies.'

'Oamaru, fair Oamaru; The port of Oamaru;
We tell you here there's nought to fear
For the port of Oamaru'

Victorian Oamaruvians liked nothing better than a sing-along. In
September 1884 'B.N.K.E.' offered townsfolk through the columns
of the North Otago Times an uplifting little ditty called 'The Port of
Oamaru'. Did its chorus catch on in the Criterion?
Did harbour board members sing it in Harbour Street?
Alas, Gentle Reader, the record is silent.

Poets Sing of heroes small and great, of battles lost and won,
They sing of almost everything extant beneath the sun;
But there is one thing they've forgot, and that we'll try to do,
'Tis this – to sing about our port, the port of Oamaru.

Oamaru, fair Oamaru;
The port of Oamaru;
We tell you here there's nought to fear
For the port of Oamaru.

Scarcely twelve months have elapsed since here we failed to get
A vessel worthy of the name to come for any freight;
Outsiders often spread reports that were not always true,
They tried to damage all they could the port of Oamaru.

Oamaru, etc.

As time rolled on our southern neighbors raved and tore their hair,
And pictured destruction to each captain who went there;
Enraged at last, a law they passed, 'twas thought they'd make us rue,
No policies they'd grant to ships that came to Oamaru.

Oamaru, etc.

Our harbor board could well afford the taunts thrown at them then.
It being composed of far the best of all our local men,
For works they planned and works they made, such splendid works they knew
Would make our port quite safe a port; three cheers for Oamaru!

Oamaru, etc.

Bold Whitson came (long live his name!) declared the works complete;
Said he, 'You can accommodate the largest in our fleet,
I'll instantly go south and bring my vessel and her crew,
And load her up for London at your port of Oamaru.'

Oamaru, etc.

The good ship came, was safely moored unto the Sumpter wharf,
The knowing ones they chuckled, and could scarcely hide a laugh;
Said they, 'We'll talk to Neptune, and a south-east storm he'll brew.
To wreck the ship Dunedin at the port of Oamaru.'

Oamaru, etc.

But to their prayers old Neptune turned a deaf and dull cold ear,
Said he, 'No harm shall come to one, my son for many a year;
Good-bye, my friends,' said Neptune old, 'that's very good for you;
My friend you do not wish to harm, but death to Oamaru.'

Oamaru, etc.

So Whitson came, and Whitson went, and said he had not found
A Safer harbor, snugger port, in all the world around;
Then next year, when Lloyd's agents his ship's polices renew,
No extra charges will they make on port of Oamaru.

Oamaru, etc.

When here the Elderslie arrives, we'll hoist our flags on high;
Songs loud and long for our harbor board will sweep across the sky.
What bold men dare, no jealousy can stop what they will do,
They ventured and they quickly made a port of Oamaru.

Oamaru, etc.

Then with a hip, hip, hip, hurrah; hurrah, hurrah, hurrah!
Our harbor board will soon complete their works without a flaw.
When parliament it next does meet, we'lltell you what they'll do, –
They'll man for man and word for word say 'Well done Oamaru.'

Oamaru, fair Oamaru;
The port of Oamaru;
We tell you here there's nought to fear
For the port of Oamaru.[43]

His shipmates responded lustily. A large crowd saw her off, cheering heartily from the wharf. Others boarded the dredge to accompany her six nautical miles out to sea, where she slipped the tow, her sails filling with a fair breeze. Oamaru's first shipment of frozen meat was on its way to British dinner tables.[43]

Her departure was timely. The *Progress* was making slow work of deepening the other Sumpter Wharf berth, so the *Elderslie* needed hers. The big ship appeared off Cape Wanbrow on Sunday 22 August, as people were leaving church, and anchored at a point off Dee Street to await the next daylight high tide. She entered port smoothly on Monday and was berthed with the help of the *Progress*. The papers praised her fittings, appointments and her forty-five crew. She had had time to load only 35 tonnes of cargo, since her charter contract required her to be at Oamaru in August. There, however, she would load 25,000 carcasses, railed from Totara Estate and from Burnside.

It was time to celebrate. It was time to be smug. In September the *Oamaru Mail* relished the chance to reprint comments from the *Timaru Herald* that epitomised Victorian New Zealand's addiction to progress, prosperity and parochialism: 'People at Oamaru appear to be doing their utmost to get ahead of their neighbouring competitors in commercial enterprise. A breakwater with a mole at the end of it, a wharf with a big hole dredged alongside, and what is more satisfactory, a big steamer lying in the big hole, loading up a huge cargo of mutton; all these things indicate progress, show a spirit of enterprise and auger well for the future prosperity of Oamaru.'[45]

The *Elderslie* loaded about 800 carcasses a day. In late September locals entertained the crew, treating them to hymns, homilies and an 'exhibition of pictures of the Mosaic Tabernacle and matters connected therewith'.[46] Loading went smoothly. The only contentious issue was the ship's contract, which specified a loaded draft of twenty feet, forcing her to detour briefly to Port Chalmers to load 300 tonnes of coal to get her to Rio de Janeiro. Nevertheless, on 14 October the *Oamaru Mail* crowed that 'the second large vessel, and the first direct steamer from this port to the Mother Country, left the Sumpter Wharf this morning at 11 o'clock with the largest cargo of frozen mutton which has ever been sent from any one port in New Zealand at any one time.'[47] The wharf was packed.

The news kept getting better that year as more refrigerated ships were announced for Oamaru: the *Marlborough* (November) and the *Turakina* (January) and it was confirmed that the *Elderslie* would leave London for Oamaru again in January 1885. Surely Sir George Grey's prophecy had come true? In 1878 the wily old flatterer had compared Oamaru to 'a fair maiden that sits upon the shores of the sea' and had compared the harbour to 'the horn of plenty'. As tall masts crowded the town's wharves and as elaborate new limestone buildings opened their doors, Oamaruvians seemed to have achieved the colonial dream.

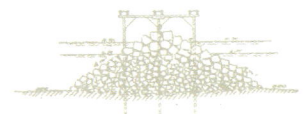

Chapter Three

'WE'LL MEND THE BREAK, AND ... WE'LL PADDLE OUR OWN CANOE',
1885–1907

Historian Felipe Fernando-Armesto argues that the most interesting history happens in port cities or in border regions of land-locked countries. By that, he means that being open to outside influences increases the likelihood of societies being dynamic and outward-looking. Victorian Oamaruvians would have understood that, for their harbour provided jobs, business, recreation, social diversions and news. The *North Otago Times* and the *Oamaru Mail* reported the daily goings-on around the wharves and their columns showed that while commerce was king, waterfront life also had a social side.

That was especially apparent during the wool season. Frozen meat steamers usually lay alongside Sumpter Wharf for just a few days, but the big sailing ships loading for London could spend a month or more. Old-timers recalled the cash and colour they brought to Tyne Street. William Bee the grocer and E. Grave the ship's chandler did good business, although they probably saw less of the sailors' brass than the publicans did. After the Northern Hotel, the Criterion and the Star & Garter closed at eleven, 'the old street resounded to sea chanties sung lustily by mixed crews from the old "wind jammers" in port.' Forty or fifty years later, 'Oamaruvian' remembered well-liquored old shellbacks pouring out of the Northern. Looking up Wansbeck Street, one spied a woman's bicycle in a doorway. Just the thing for a joyride! But he got more than he bargained for. Wansbeck Street is steep and the bicycle gathered speed as it descended. 'Port your helm, Bill' or 'starboard, Bill, starboard', the sailor's friends called out nautically, but he hit the kerb and skidded along the footpath into Oyster Ben's fish stall, sending red cod, flounder and groper flying. Ben's language was as salty as his goods, but 'a return to the Northern eventually had its compensations for both of them and all misunderstandings were washed out in a lead pot or two.'[1]

Sailors' misdeeds were usually limited to drunkenness and horseplay, surprising given the harsh conditions under which they laboured, and the deficiencies of some of their

Ships waited for sheep. On 11 December 1893 the New Zealand Shipping Co's barque Waipa *(1057 tons, left) was swung off the wharf to allow the Union Company's Sydney steamer* Wakatipu *(1792 tons) to discharge coal and wool. The* Waipa *and Shaw Savill & Albion's* Pleiades *(1020 tons right) had arrived in Oamaru on 11 and 17 November respectively to load wool for London, the* Pleiades *coming via the Cape, and the* Waipa *via Timaru. On 31 December the* North Otago Times *reported that the* Pleiades *had sailed two days earlier for London 'with a fair wind. There has been uninterrupted fine weather for the shearing, and the* Pleiades *has met with quick despatch, the wool coming forward continuously.' The* Waipa *was expected to sail for London on 5 January.*

– North Otago Museum 280

officers. In December 1882, in a rare case, a magistrate sentenced Seaman T. Hillman to fourteen days' hard labour for disobeying the instructions of the master of the barque *Unicorn*. A quarrel between Hillman and the second mate had escalated into a stand-up fight. The magistrate 'was determined to show that the discipline of the captain of a vessel must be maintained', but told the captain to reprove his second mate for throwing a handspike at Hillman.[2]

Oamaruvians paid close attention to ships, especially the big 'Home' boats. In January 1888 on a fine summer evening, the Oamaru City Band gave a promenade concert aboard the *Fifeshire*, a frequent visitor in the 1880s and the 1890s. That evening townsfolk danced beneath the stars and the lights rigged up for the occasion.[3] When the *Nairnshire* visited in May 1890, 'large numbers of people took the opportunity of visiting and inspecting the vessel, which the affability of the officers rendered agreeable.'[4] Unfortunately, not all visits went smoothly. When Shaw Savill & Albion's *Mamari* was opened to the public in February 1891, visitors committed 'acts of wanton destruction that even a larrikin would have every reason to feel ashamed of,' cutting their initials into the deckhouses' woodwork, severing a large manila hawser and smoking in the saloon. Oamaruvians were too much for the captain, who said that was the last time he would

open the ship to the public there.[5] The weather was no kinder to him. Just before sailing, a storm caught the *Mamari* at the wharf, buckling fittings and damaging wharf fender piles. He must have been delighted to hit the open sea.

Visiting warships also provided welcome diversions. In January 1892 the cruiser HMS *Ringarooma* paid a courtesy call. Captain Edmund Bourke wrote to the mayor in advance to say that he planned to open her to visitors. The Oamaru Navals prepared for a concert. They boarded the cruiser, but soon afterwards, a gale sprang up and the ship broke a mooring, compelling Bourke to put to sea. The Navals spent an unexpected night in hammocks, but seem to have enjoyed the experience, and were rowed back by boat next morning. To compensate Oamaruvians deprived of their visit and concert, the *Ringarooma* played her searchlight over the town. Farmers reported seeing it from several kilometres inland.[6]

Engineers like to spend money. In October 1884, just days after the *Elderslie* had sailed, McGregor

---

Gunboat diplomacy. HMS Ringdove *lies off Sumpter Wharf in May 1893, showing the flag. Lieutenant-commander E. Bain brought the 805-ton ship from Dunedin on a goodwill voyage.* Ringdove *carried six 4-inch guns, two 3-prs and had a crew of 76 officers and men. – North Otago Museum 2847*

MESSING ABOUT IN BOATS

It was not just merchants and master mariners who welcomed the breakwater and the mole. So did Oamaru's frustrated boaties. An open roadstead was no place for pleasure craft.

At a meeting of the Oamaru Yachting Club in February 1875, 'in consequence of the Club not being able to keep a yacht at the port, on account of there being no anchorage where she could lie at her moorings in security, and the Club having completed the purchase of a lifeboat' [the ship *Auckland*'s 8.2-metre lifeboat], the club changed its name to the Oamaru Boating Club. It also altered its aims to encouraging boating in general and to training a crew to assist shipwrecked mariners.[7] Oars, not sails, would dominate recreational boating until well into the twentieth century.

The history of recreational boating at Oamaru is murky, to put it charitably. Did the OBC expire, or did it change its name to the Oamaru Union Rowing Club? In 1986 the Oamaru Rowing Club (Inc) published a centenary booklet that mentioned an 1887 OURC AGM decision to work with the Railway Boating Club to secure a site for a shed. A tender was let in November of that year to D. Smart and two years later another AGM voted to move the shed closer to the mole. In November 1887, Edward Lane, the OURC secretary, wrote to the *North Otago Times* to say that despite rumours that only youths and boys were admitted to membership 'we are quite willing to admit anybody, be they as old as Methusaleh.'[8]

In 1898, in a report of the OURC's AGM, chairman P. Evans described the past season as the club's best since its formation in 1885, despite having to relocate the clubhouse after the shingle accumulated in front of the shed. The forty members who attended the 1900 AGM at the Star & Garter learned that their club's accounts were balanced, thirty new members had been approved, and the committee had ordered 'a four-oared racing boat and two four-oared practice tubs and also a stock of new oars.' And it had also added to the clubhouse. Next year the Oamaru Boating Club applied to join the New Zealand Amateur Rowing Association. It opened new premises in 1903.

In addition to regular club activities, there were occasional yacht races between Otago and Oamaru harbours and regattas within the harbour. One took place in May 1885, blessed with such fine weather that even the pulling boats could use the course off the harbour. The *Dunedin* was in port, so she became the regatta flagship.

There were more events than boats. In the ten-mile race for sailing boats, Oamaru boat *Aid* beat Moeraki boat *Pinafore* after the *Nautilus* broke her mast-head. In the fishing boat race, the same pair battled it out over a four-mile course. In the open boat sailing race, the *Kakanui* squeaked in between *Aid* and *Pinafore* for second prize. In the senior four-oar in-rig gig race, the Timaru boat *Otipua* beat the *Enchantress*, the *Wild Rose* and *Maori Chief* failing to start. The Navals dominated the four-oar ships' gig race.

Sailors from the ships in port also entered several races, including the four-oar gig race. In the race for youths under twenty, the order was *Clifton*, *Jane*, *Dunedin* and *Takapuna*. In the open category, rowed over two miles, the *Clifton*'s crew beat the *Dunedin*'s.

Women competed for prizes, not cash, but goods: 'brooch and earrings, given by Mr Cathcart: silver bracelet, given by Mr Ricketts; and gold locket, given by Messrs G and T Young. Winning boat to have choice of prizes.' In the women's sculling race, Miss A. Ward in *Rose* led from the beginning, beating Miss E. Ward in the *Maggie* by a dozen lengths.

Gin palace. This impressive steam launch is a visitor – Oamaruvians never owned anything that large. The photograph also shows a 'smack', as racing craft were called, powering in under all sail. – North Otago Museum 985

Shipping a green one. The photographer captures a wave breaking over the breakwater while a barquentine swings at her moorings in its lee. In very bad storms such as in 1886, waves covered the entire structure. – North Otago Museum 294

urged dredging the harbour to 7.3 metres at low water (£30,000). Since the *Progress* was not up to this, he recommended buying an 800-tonne hopper capacity steam dredge (£27,000) to minimise steaming time. More wharves would be needed (five new ones for £30,000) and he also recommended rock-armouring the seaward edge of the breakwater (£4000) and building the mole's concrete head (£3000). His wish list totalled £94,000, rounded up to £100,000 (over $15 million in 2007 dollars) after contingencies.

Fat chance! The board was broke, although the warning about dredging was timely. Amongst the fanfares and celebrations of that year, the Union Company steamers *Hawea* and the *Tekapo* sounded cautionary notes. On 30 July 1884, the *Hawea* touched on a spit of shingle off the breakwater head. She was not damaged, but the timing – just before the arrival of the *Elderslie* – drove the *Oamaru Mail* to explain a trifle ingenuously that the dredge was about to remove the shingle and that the warning buoy that should have obviated the incident had been blown away. Then in September 1884, the *Tekapo* (2439 tons) stranded while entering port at half-tide at 0630. Recent storms had pushed the shingle bank off the breakwater head into the channel, reducing the depth from 5.2 metres feet at low water to 4.3–4.6 metres. Fortunately, the shingle was soft, the sea was calm and the tide was on the rise, enabling the *Tekapo* to float off and berth by 0115. No damage was done, but the incident reinforced the need for caution after

Rough Sea. Breakwater. Oamaru.   J.M.B.

storms. Although Oamaru was now a safe, well-protected harbour, nothing could be taken for granted.[9]

Silting was less of a problem than storm damage. Heavy seas had damaged the breakwater several times during construction, so it was inevitable that Neptune would try to do his worst after its completion. The heavy ENE storm that hit on Saturday 14 August 1886 was exceptional. It raged for days, gathering in malevolent intensity. By Tuesday, massive green seas covered the breakwater, alarming Thomas Forrester, who could make out only fleeting glimpses of the structure through the driving rain and the crashing waves and spray. Already he had seen enough to be worried. On Wednesday, first light revealed the elevated rail tracks used to build the

breakwater wrecked and hanging loose. Unfortunately, the seas were still too violent to permit closer inspection, but the signs were not good. On Thursday morning the sea could be observed boiling up noisily under the monoliths about 150–160 metres from the end. On 28 August a southerly storm caused more damage. In the short interval between storms, Forrester discovered that the waves had displaced the outer upper blocks between sections 20 and 28 and had broken up the monolith at section 26. There was now a 100-metre gap in the breakwater; unless the board acted quickly, it risked losing the entire structure.

The timing could not have been worse. The board had overstretched itself and had balanced its books in 1885 only by selling surplus cement, precisely the material it now needed, and in big quantities. It had also dismissed Captain Shand, its pilot, and laid off the dredge night watchman and the general night watchman. The worried dredge master reported that his crew had 'absolutely' refused to act as night watchmen aboard the vessel, which had already broken from her moorings during the night, hitting Sumpter Wharf. Captain Joseph Pallant, the lighthouse keeper and port signalman, also jibbed at being told to become night watchman as well as signalman. 'The board surely do not expect me to act as night watchman from 6 p.m. to 6 a.m., as per your note, and as signalman from daylight till dark as per my present instructions', he asked with incredulity.[10]

So, the board faced hard decisions. Dropping the outer edge armouring had clearly been a false economy and would have to be rectified. But how would it pay for the work? It halted dredging and issued tenders for

A barquentine lies at the inner moorings in the afternoon sun, either awaiting cargo or moved to make way for another ship (note the rail wagons on Sumpter Wharf). Even the relatively gentle swell breaks right across the breakwater.
– North Otago Museum 1886

2862 — BREAKWATER - OAMARU.

One of the Burton Bros' signature photographs from the mid-1880s: big overseas ships lie at or just off Sumpter Wharf, the spindly mast of the Dunedin ferry Beautiful Star peer over the west side of Normanby Wharf, a barque lies at the Macandrew Wharf outer berth and a rake of wagons sits on the Cross Wharf waiting for its ship to come in. The breakwater is now complete and the steam crane 'Moa' is parked at its landward end (left) where it eventually rusted away.
– Alexander Turnbull Library C-22767-1/2

BURTON BROS. DUNEDIN

THE RUSSIANS ARE COMING?

On a fine day in April 1885, 400 Dunedin excursionists aboard the Union Company's Hawea *found themselves part of the drama they had come to watch. 'On nearing the scene of action at about 1 o'clock, the attacking squadron was first sighted – the vessels lying about a cable's length apart, and no doubt busily engaged in clearing their decks for action', the* Otago Witness *reported.*

'The *Hinemoa* (flagship) was at the extremity of the line nearest to the harbour entrance, the *Beautiful Star* lay next, then the tug *Plucky*, and on the left of the line the Union Company's *Ohau* and the Harbour Board's launch *Reynolds*. The *Hawea*, steaming innocently along to see the fun, was greeted by a shot across her bows from the *Hinemoa*, which some of the excursionists took as a complimentary salute, the number of guns being perhaps curtailed from motives of economy. But this was not the case. A boatload of navals suddenly shot out from somewhere and pulled in a most determined and muscular manner in the direction of the *Hawea*. Arrived alongside (for Captain Hansby disdained to seek safety in flight), they elevated their oars man-o'-war fashion, and the commanding officer addressed the captain on his own bridge with considerable curtness, presumably calling upon him to surrender or walk the plank. There is reason to believe that the disappointing action of the *Hawea*'s commander upon this occasion was forced upon him by outside pressure. His natural inclination must have been to reply that there were British colours above his head, a British ship beneath his feet, and that he should fight her while two planks held together, and then ignite the powder magazine and disappear gracefully with his crew in fragments. But Captain Hansby resisted this impulse, probably remembering that there was no powder magazine on board; and having surrendered to the enterprising navals, was permitted to proceed alongside the wharf and land his passengers, who were made to suffer none of the inconveniences of captivity. It should be explained on behalf of the excursionists that they scarcely understood the hostile purpose of the boarding party during the few moments they remained alongside, or they would have pitched boots, and parasols, and soda water bottles into the boat and harassed the enemy not a little.'[11]

SKETCHES OF BOMBARDMENT OF OAMARU

The day-trippers had come to see the Easter encampment at Oamaru, where the mainland's professional and volunteer soldiers practised defending the town. It was not entirely academic. Britain had just passed through one of its periodic Russian scares and a year earlier, at the height of the Russian scare, Colonel Henry Cautley had batted back Oamaru requests for coastal defence guns with the 'helpful' suggestion that if a raider appeared, the town's inhabitants should refuse to give anything except under protest, to remove all valuables inland and destroy coal supplies.[12] Only the main ports were defended. Coastal defence in places such as Oamaru was carried out by volunteers. *Defending New Zealand* notes that in 1878 there was a 24-pounder howitzer at Oamaru. It was in the care of the Oamaru Artillery Volunteers, formed three years earlier, but renamed I Battery of the New Zealand Regiment of Volunteer Artillery in 1878. Like all such units, it used obsolete weapons, listed as three 24-pdr howitzers from 1887 and three 9-pdr RMLs by 1893.[13] There was also an Oamaru Naval Artillery Volunteers Unit, formed in January 1884. In December of that year the government steamer *Stella* landed a gun for this unit. It was ancient, an old muzzle-loader dating from the reign of King George III in 1812. But that mattered not a jot to the men of the unit, who sang marching songs as they hauled the two-and-a-half tonne gun from the good shed to the esplanade.[14] The Volunteers, as these units were called, held inter-district encampments most years in each island. In 1886 Oamaru hosted the mainland's. It was a showstopper, recorded for posterity by Dunedin photographers the Burton Brothers and by water colourist C. Aubrey, albeit with more enthusiasm than artistic talent or even sense of perspective. The encampment lasted for four days, 2551 men camping on the

racecourse for four days. The tea and coffee were 'inferior', but after some adjustments, space was found in the grandstand and outbuildings for those without tents. The press spoke of two 400-gallon iron tanks brewing tea, a four-horsepower engine to steam the vegetables, and of the troops chomping through 500 kg of meat for breakfast, 1000 kg for dinner and another 500 kg served cold for tea. Although 'some of the cooks looked as if they would have benefited greatly from a wash', the food, though plain, was adequate.

Hundreds of spectators flooded into the town to enjoy the Easter show, cramming into the parlours, dining rooms and even billiard rooms of the town's hotels and boarding houses. Oamaru was bursting at the seams. It was estimated that over 10,000 people watched the show.

Most accounts praised the weather, the behaviour of the men and the organisation of the camp. The *Otago Witness*'s reporter was a little less effusive. 'What strikes a visitor most is the great want of discipline in camp,' he grumbled. 'The straw for bedding is scrambled for, bugles are blown without authority, and the men

---

Above: Excursion steamer Hawea *and frozen meat ship* Dunedin *at Sumpter Wharf, while the* Hinemoa, Beautiful Star, Plucky *and* Ohau, *off the crowded breakwater, represent 'attacking' forces. – Burton Bros, Alexander Turnbull Library F-60840-1/2*

Opposite top: Artist G.F. Fodor sketched the highlights of the mock attack, complete with detonating submarine mines. – G.F. Fodor, Alexander Turnbull Library

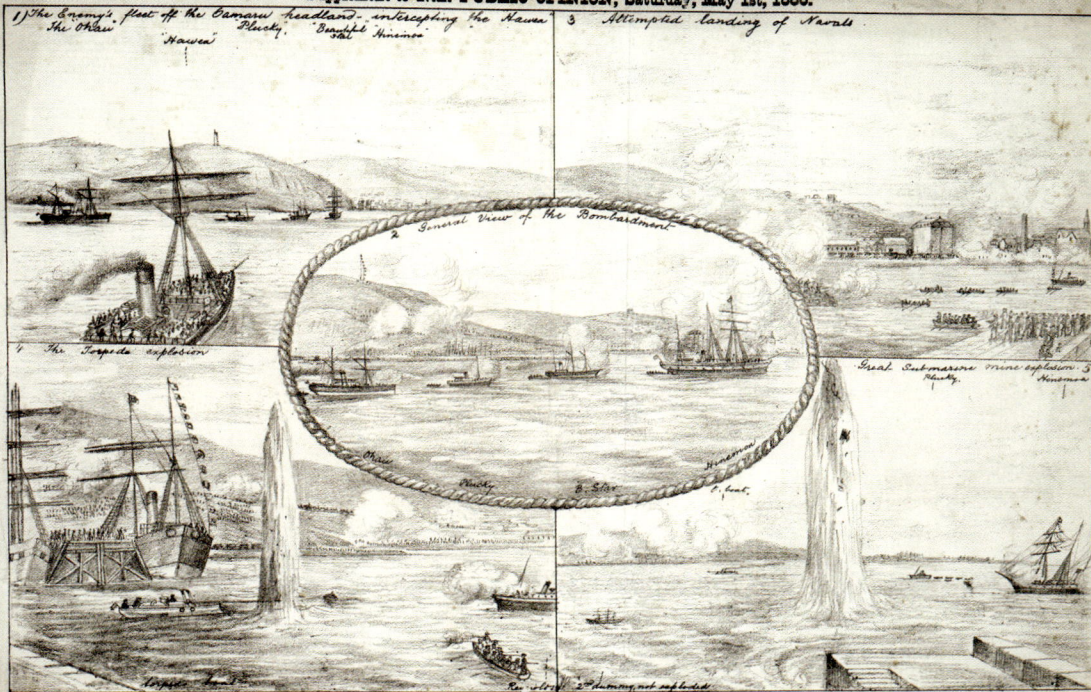

SKETCHES OF BOMBARDMENT OF OAMARU.
By our Special Artist, Mr. G. F. FODOR.

wander about the camp singing and skylarking till all hours in the morning. Numbers of the men also steal away from camp and go into town without leaves as the shades of night descend.' But they were saints compared to the town's mercenary cab drivers. The *Witness's* man moaned about being asked to pay 7s 6d to be taken the short distance out to the camp site and later that evening saw members of the Dunedin B Battery bargaining with a hansom-driver to take them out for £1 ($160 in today's terms).[15]

Rear-admiral Scott R.N commanded the attacking forces. There were several actions: a naval attack, a review and a 'sham fight'. The naval attack was the highlight. The *Hinemoa* led the assault, followed by the other ships, engaging shore batteries. The *Plucky* and the *Reynolds* forced their way into harbour, providing covering fire for the landing boats. Next was the star of the show, *No. 169*, the little Thorneycroft torpedo boat from Port Chalmers. 'The speed the boat was driven at was tremendous, being fully 17½ knots per hour, and the easy way she was handled, turing in a space almost her own length' amazed onlookers, the *Timaru Herald* reported, as the slate-grey-coloured steamer rushed towards the *Reynolds*, 'exploding a torpedo within a short distance of that ill-starred launch.' The *Hinemoa* and the ships outside the harbour withdrew, pursued by the torpedo boat: 'She closed upon the *Plucky* relentlessly and passed from her to others of the squadron, inflicting an amount of damage that was left to the imagination.' The attackers returned, emboldened by silencing the batteries on the Cape, and pressed closer to the harbour. 'But here occurred the final catastrophe – the explosion from the shore of a submarine mine which had been laid to protect the entrance of the harbour', the *Witness* reported. An old surf boat had been rigged and fitted up to look like a ship:

'This was really a magnificent spectacle – a bulky column of water being thrown at least 150ft or 200ft into the air, carrying with it a mass of *debris* which a few minutes before had been a dummy boat placed there … This casualty – by which he must have lost one or other of his vessels – finally discomforted the gallant admiral: he was in the language of his own instructions, 'shattered,' and he steamed alongside the wharf, not to receive his 400,000 florins, but to shake hands with the his friend the enemy – the colonel commandant, and ask why mine No. 1 had not been exploded as agreed upon. It seemed that the *Hinemoa's* propeller had cut the wire connecting this mine to the shore, and thus averted the destruction of at least one of the squadron. So the engagement ended, in the only way it could end, without seriously injuring the *amour propre* of our volunteers. It was undoubtedly a most brilliant attack while it lasted, and the defence was equally spirited. The spectators were vastly interested in the spectacle, and no doubt gained an excellent idea of what such an attack would really be like if made by vessels carrying no heavier ordnance than the *Hinemoa* on board'.[16]

The weekend passed almost without incident. A corporal was injured when a gun carriage wheel came off and hit his leg and a local man had a fright while attending to business aboard the *Dunedin* at Sumpter Wharf. When the guns fired, his horse broke away and thundered towards Normanby Wharf, trailing a trap. The panicked animal hurtled along the wharf and seemed destined to plunge into the harbour, trap and all, when two men caught and calmed it at the last moment.[17]

new concrete blocks, but had no money for the actual repairs, estimated to cost £30,000 (including £22,000 for armouring). The government ignored pleas to subsidise a work claimed to be of national significance. It also brushed aside suggestions that it should have paid three times the £9300 it had given for land taken for railway purposes. Oamaru was on its own.

The Athenaeum was packed on 10 December to debate borrowing £30,000. It was an emotional issue, and Sumpter and Shrimski made their pitch, Sumpter bringing along a pre-printed speech to hand out to indignant ratepayers. When asked why the board had not made the wall shorter and thicker, he replied that small harbours made no sense as a short breakwater would have made the harbour 'much smaller – a mere coffin – to bury their hopes in.'[18] When people moved and seconded the motion that 'the Harbor Board retire altogether', Sumpter ignored this inconvenient outbreak of democracy and kept talking, calling for unity and offering a tune he had composed walking down the street that night:

> We'll help each other all we can,
> And our good town, Oamaru;
> We'll mend the break, and man to man,
> We'll paddle our own canoe.

Sentiment, not poetic quality helped him carry the day. People were angry about being asked to pay higher rates, but no one wanted to jeopardise the harbour, widely seen as the key to the district's prosperity. So they grumbled and they asked pointed questions, but they put their hands in their pockets. Around North Otago, meetings backed the loan: twenty out of twenty-eight voting for it at Pukeuri, a unanimous vote at Molloy's Hotel, Sandhurst, and so on.

David Miller, familiar with the breakwater, started on the protection work in July 1887. It was not easy. A diver's services were essential for much of the time, but sea conditions prevented him from submerging about one day in two, on average. Miller repaired the first large monolith in January 1888. Workers started at three in the morning and had the caisson filled up by late that afternoon.[19] It was his swansong. Two months later he died of cancer, leaving his wife to complete the contract. Then the cement supplier went bankrupt. Next, the contractor for the next stage of the project, A. Watson died, leaving his widow responsible for a contract she could not complete. It was cancelled by mutual consent, and work resumed under the direction of Thomas Forrester and the board's inspector of works.[20] It was finished by the end of 1889.

In 1890, Oamaru got caught up with the Maritime Strike, the first of the great waterfront disputes that coloured our wider political history. The dispute originated in Australia and was heightened when the Union Company objected to the ships' officers' union, the N.Z. Merchant Service Guild, joining the Maritime Council, an umbrella grouping of transport and associated workers. The dispute broke out in mid-August and lasted until early November.

Oamaru became involved only in the second week of September, when two large ships arrived. The first, the Union Company's *Wakatipu*, left on the tenth with 3000 sacks of grain for Sydney, loaded by non-union labour after the Maritime Council called out the local union. A similar call went to the men working the British sailing ship *Margaret Galbraith*. On 13 September Arthur Warren, secretary of the Oamaru branch of the Waterside Lumpers' Union (as wharfies were known then), thanked the ship's crew for refusing to strike-break: 'the sailors stated that they were British seamen, and would not act as such; and further, that they were Union men, and not blacklegs.' But the employers brought in 'free labour' ('scabs' to the unionists) and although the new men worked less efficiently, and at first only one ship could be worked at a time, they kept cargo moving.

The record of the dispute is hazy. The local papers took an anti-union line, although it was interesting that the *North Otago Times*'s 15 September editorial noted that 'at nearly all the ports, with the prominent exceptions of Oamaru and Timaru, men have been found to do the work of the lumpers, not so well, perhaps, as the regular hands, but still it is done,' indicating union resilience. Two days earlier, Warren had advertised a meeting of the 'old Oamaru Lumpers' Union' would be held at the hut on the wharf that morning. That and a casual reference to the *Silver Cloud* being worked by 'union labour', suggested that while a new union may have been formed, the members of the old one stayed staunch. On 3 November, in the dying days of the strike, a deputation from the Oamaru union asked the Union Company's port agent to take them back on en masse. They were told that that the men must apply individually and that it would be in their interests to sever their connection with the Maritime Council. At a meeting later that day, the men decided unanimously not to return to work 'except in a body.'[21] The *Wakatipu* was back in port, being worked by non-union labour from Dunedin. But less than a week later, Oamaru labour was working the coaster *Brunner*; the strike was over and the Maritime Council was defeated.

A Southland visitor who inspected the breakwater in 1889 was very impressed by what he saw: 'it is a "concrete: declaration of the fact that for a mercantile people harbor means city and no harbor no city'.[22] But the harbour's finances were built on sand, which in 1891 made a seismic shift. The board had traded on a knife edge for years and an accumulation of relatively minor blows – the loss of the old Dunedin ferry trade due to railway competition, rabbit damage to its Otematata estate, reduced rentals on its town properties, the prolonged 'Long Depression', the impact of the Maritime Strike and the drought's reduction in export volumes – tipped it over the edge. In 1890 a crisis was averted only by reaching a temporary accommodation with the government. But the fundamentals remained unsound, and in October 1891 the board told the London bondholders of the 1879 loan the bad news that it would default on the November interest payments.

Reaction was hostile. In the North Island, the New Plymouth Harbour Board was also floundering, so sympathy was limited.

The *Evening Post* said Oamaru's history 'affords striking proof of the folly – we might almost write criminality – of the policy which, when the colony had decided on borrowing largely for the construction of arterial lines of land communication, permitted public bodies to be created with powers to borrow money with which to

OAMARU HARBOR BOARD.

REPORT

AND

STATEMENTS OF ACCOUNTS

BALANCE-SHEET FOR THE YEAR ENDED 31st DECEMBER, 1889.

I.—GENERAL ACCOUNT.

RECEIPTS.	£ s. d.	£ s. d.
Transferred from Interest Account No. 4		643 2 4
Transferred from Interest Account No. 5		1,494 12 3
ESTATE—		
Outstanding Rents—31st Dec., 1888 ..	749 2 6	
Town Rents accrued	2,031 5 0	
Otematata Rent accrued	3,085 0 0	
	5,865 7 6	
Less Outstanding, 31st Dec., 1889 ..	559 2 6	
		5,306 5 0
Repairs to Roads refunded by Tenants..		26 5 0
WHARF WORKING—		
Outstanding Accounts—31st Dec., 1888	1,074 10 10	
Wharfage Dues	5,546 5 8	
Berthage	1,276 13 4	
Warps	774 11 1	
Cranage	271 0 8	
Ballast	28 4 0	
Water	95 0 6	
	9,067 6 1	
Less Outstanding, 31st Dec., 1889 ..	718 11 2	
		8,348 14 11
HARBOR—		
Lighthouse Reserve Rents, 31st Dec., 1888	7 10 0	
Lighthouse Reserve Rents accrued ..	26 5 0	
	33 15 0	
Less Outstanding, 31st Dec., 1889 ..	16 5 0	
	17 10 0	
Port Fees	688 14 2	
Pilotage	664 8 6	
Removal Fees	4 2 11	
Pilotage Exemption Certificates ..	35 18 0	
Boat License	2 0 0	
		1,412 13 7
SUNDRY RECEIPTS—		
Cash for Towage of Vessels ..	89 0 0	
Cash for Old Iron	19 13 9	
		108 13 9
		17,340 6 10
Balance, 31st Dec., 1889		4,282 15 1
		£21,623 1 11

EXPENDITURE.	£ s. d.	£ s. d.
Balance, 31st December, 1888		2,582 15 4
Transferred to Interest Account No. 1 ..		3,900 0 0
Transferred to Interest Account No. 2 ..		1,925 0 0
Transferred to Interest Account No. 3 ..		6,000 0 0
Transferred to Sinking Fund Acct. No. 1		650 0 0
Transferred to Sinking Fund Acct. No. 2		350 0 0
Bank Interest on Overdraft		125 7 0
ESTATE—		
Wages and Accounts, Repairs to Roads	23 12 4	
Borough Rates on Unoccupied Sections	4 14 6	
Hislop and Creagh, Expenses re Leases	23 4 0	
Fleming and Hedley, Expenses re Leases	7 10 0	
Live Stock Department, Ferrets.. ..	24 11 3	
Accounts	6 1 0	
		89 13 1
WHARF WORKING—		
Wages	606 10 4	
Renewals and Repairs	565 17 5	
Ballast	11 18 6	
Coal	20 5 9	
Expenses	29 12 6	
Ry. Commission, Collection of Dues ..	145 4 11	
		1,379 9 5
HARBOR—		
Harbormaster, Lightkeeper, and Wages to Men	719 2 5	
Accounts	292 14 10	
		1,011 17 3
PERMANENT WORKS—		
Ordinary Repairs to Works		36 11 0
DREDGING—		
Wages	1,585 2 1	
Coal	386 0 1	
Insurance	305 4 9	
Customs Certificate	6 0 0	
Accounts	555 18 5	
		2,838 5 4
EXPENSES—		
Secretary and Assistant (quota) ..	160 17 1	
Ordinary and Office Expenses ..	205 18 4	
Expenses and Clerical Work re Rates ..	165 15 5	
Expenses re Loan	10 11 8	
Expenses re Election	6 9 9	
Bank Commission and Exchange ..	184 11 3	
		734 3 6
		£21,623 1 11

attempt the construction of artificial harbours to compete with the State railways.'[23] That was going too far – the port had halved the freights charged between Dunedin and Oamaru and had expanded its trade. The problem, however, was that it had no liquidity. Loan servicing was a financial black hole, sucking up everything.

From London, the *Financial News* blamed the board for constructing 'works quite beyond the needs of their business ... in the true colonial way'.[24] The board remitted money when it could, but by 1893 was £12,000 in arrears. That year the 1879 bondholders applied to the Supreme Court for an order and the board's revenue was put in the charge of the court, which appointed as receiver the Trustees, Executors and Agency Company of New Zealand. It had full control over the board's finances. It had to approve the purchase of every bag of cement, mooring rope and dredge repair.

Although the board's debt continued to accumulate, the second half of the 1890s saw the colony shrug off the Long Depression. Subdivision of the big pastoral estates also brought increased trade for the port, as more intensive farming produced more exports. The turn of the century brought a brief windfall, the South African ('Boer') War. Imperial troops and horses needed food and supplies, so a procession of ships unfamiliar to Oamaruvians shuttled in and out of the harbour, loading grain for South Africa. It lasted for two years. The ships – the *Claverdon, Star of Victoria, Kilburn, Annerly, Werneth Hall, Spithead* and

Border Knight, amongst others in 1900 – were big, and at times the harbour presented a busy sight, especially if a grain ship was loading at the same time as a frozen meat carrier. The 112-metre four-masted steamer *Werneth Hall* severely taxed Sumpter Wharf.

Another South African War spin-off reinforced the harbour's inadequacies. Late in 1900 the government advertised tenders for a scheduled shipping service between Australasia and South Africa, but its requirement for 4000-ton register ships excluded Oamaru from the ports' schedule. The *North Otago Times* hoped that occasionally Oamaru might be made the first port of call on the outward trip, since the ships would not be too deeply laden at that stage, but accepted that Sumpter Wharf was not up to handling ships of this class.[25]

The South African grain trade had gone completely by 1902. The frozen meat trade remained, but here, too, ship size growth was causing problems. In 1903 the *Turakina* became the last sailing ship to load a UK cargo at Oamaru. Soon the first generation steamers were also going to the breakers, replaced by larger ships, many too large for Sumpter Wharf. By the early 1900s, the *Elderslie*, considered a big ship in 1884, was smaller than some coastal and trans-Tasman steamers calling at Oamaru.

Even the biggest of the dwindling number of Home boats that could still use the port taxed its facilities. In January 1895, the New Zealand Shipping Company's chartered steamer *Duke of Westminster* had set a port

THE *TILIKUM*

'The next morning after leaving Dunedin we sighted Oamaru, a small town situated near the beach. Coming nearer, we saw an artificial breakwater, inside of which a large vessel lay alongside a wharf. Near that ship I brought the Tilikum *up, and as place and people also looked inviting, we remained for a few days.'*[26]

One of Oamaru's smallest visitors was also one of its most interesting. In 1901, Canadians Captain John Voss and journalist Kenny Luxton decided to emulate American Joshua Slocum's recent round-the-world voyage in the sloop *Spray*, popularised in 1899 by his best-seller *Sailing Alone Around the World*. Voss did not sail single-handed (or at least not intentionally), so his bid for fame was based on sailing the smallest possible craft. The *Tilikum* (Chinook for 'friend') was literally a canoe, built from a single cedar log, dug-out in traditional style. Even when decked over and given a keel by Voss, the craft was tiny, 11.6 metres in length overall and 1.7 metres across. With the addition of two (one for part of the journey) crew, half a tonne of ballast and 'three months' provisions, consisting mostly of tinned goods; one camera; two rifles; one double-barrelled shot gun; one revolver; ammunition; barometer and navigating instruments', the *Tilikum*

Captain John Voss's famous round-the-world canoe Tilikum lies off the mole in March 1903. – Weekly Press photograph, Bishop collection, Canterbury Museum, Ref 1923.53.532

still drew just 0.6 metres forward and a fraction less aft.[27] Three spindly little masts provided the motive power. Voss and Luxton set out from Victoria, British Columbia, on 27 May 1901. Three years, three months and twelve days later, on 2 September 1904 the *Tilikum* tied up at Margate in the United Kingdom, cheered by thousands. Along the way, sailing novice Luxton had abandoned the voyage under 'strained' circumstances in Fiji and his replacement was swept overboard in a storm.

The New Zealand leg of the voyage of 'the 40,000-mile canoe' was less dramatic and involved a northwards journey up the coast after making landfall at Bluff on 21 February 1903. Oamaruvians had read about the *Tilikum*'s big-send off from Otago Harbour and were waiting on the mole in the early hours of the following

morning to greet the little boat as she rounded the breakwater. Voss earned his keep by lecturing as he went, so next day he had the *Tilikum* lifted from the water and displayed on a carriage in front of a department store to promote 'the only chance the public will have of seeing the smallest ship that ever reached New Zealand.'[28] His Saturday evening lecture on his trans-Pacific voyage was well attended – so much so that the amount he raised at Oamaru (£30) was not far short of his take at Dunedin (£50). The *Tilikum* sailed for Timaru on Monday 30 March.

Voss, who died in San Francisco in 1922, forty years before Luxton, never quite edged Slocum from his pedestal, but the epic story of the *Tilikum*'s round-the-world voyage remains in print as a yachting classic.

Full house. The South African War brought a welcome stream of tramp ships loading grain to feed army horses. This undated and unidentified photograph probably dates from then. A big tramp is loading at the western berth. The Home boat closer to the camera is the New Zealand Shipping Co's Tekoa (4050 tons), which visited Oamaru several times while in NZSCo service between 1890 and 1902. – North Otago Museum 2377

THE *FIFESHIRE* GROUNDS OFF BUSHY BEACH

*Nothing larger than a fishing vessel has been
wrecked at Oamaru since 1879.*

But one big Home boat was almost lost off Cape Wanbrow in 1895. Ever since the arrival of the *Elderslie*, the steamers of the Scottish Shire Line had had a special bond with Oamaru. One, the *Fifeshire*, was a regular visitor to Oamaru for a decade from 1887. As we saw, she once served as a concert/dance venue alongside Sumpter Wharf and a few years later she pulled the end of the same wharf out of alignment while berthed there in a storm.

In the early hours of 7 December 1895, the *Fifeshire* arrived off Otago Heads on a voyage from London via Sydney. She was ordered to Oamaru, where she arrived in the roadstead at 2100 hours. As it was dark and misty, and there was a heavy swell running, she was not brought in and began steaming slowly off Cape Wanbrow, waiting for conditions to improve. At 0030 hours the next morning she touched a reef opposite Bushy Beach and stuck fast.

The crew fired distress rockets and sounded the siren, but the thick fog and the bulk of the Cape prevented the rockets from being seen in the town. Some people heard her siren, but did not associate it with a distress signal.

Fortunately a man who lived near the Cape walked into town and aroused Captain Sewell, who set out in an open boat. Sewell found nothing, and thinking the ship may have sailed for Port Chalmers, returned to port. At 0500 hours, however, the *Fifeshire* was seen off the breakwater. Sewell boarded her and anchored her out in deeper water.[29] She had had a narrow escape, considering the heavy sea running. After failing to free his ship by reversing engines, Captain Wilson had pumped out the water ballast and jettisoned 50 tonnes of coal, lightening her sufficiently to float free on the rising tide. Since it was impossible to reduce her draft to allow for the two-metre swell running at the entrance, Sewell returned with two passengers, the ship's doctor and Mrs William Lang, an Oamaru resident returning to town. The *Fifeshire* docked at Lyttelton, escorted by the tug *Koputai*.

Four years later, on 15 September 1899, the coastal steamer *Pareora* clipped the edge of a reef off Cape Wanbrow. The court of inquiry blamed the master for failing to take bearings when setting the course and the mate for failing to summon him when the weather grew hazy.

length record of 121.9 metres.[30] Unfortunately Sumpter Wharf was looking rather tired. In the same year, Captain Sewell had drawn the board's attention to the fact that several years previously the *Fifeshire* had pulled the end of the wharf out of alignment by twenty metres. In 1901. Forrester recommended widening and strengthening it.

But the board had no money, so they waited and watched. By 1903 the port's limitations were being discussed in the press. Some wanted to abolish the harbour board and hand its assets to the Farmers' Union. In May 1903, the papers reported that the 151-metre long freighter *Essex* had bypassed Oamaru because she was drawing over six metres. Noting that the swinging basin would have been 15 metres too short to turn the ship even had she squeezed in, the *North Otago Times* joked that 'it might have been preferable to swing that vessel opposite the gas works, for there she might have served the purpose of acting as a breakwater, and prevented, for some time at least, the erosion of the sea.'[31]

The issues came to a head in 1903 after Captain James Ramsay, who had become harbourmaster after Sewell retired in 1896 (he died the following year), struggled to berth the *Maori*. The *North Otago Times* told readers that Ramsay had 'no greater difficulty in berthing the *Maori*

than he has any other vessel,' but the experience put him off berthing ships longer than 400 feet (121.9 metres). The board was aghast, but once word got out about his *Maori* ultimatum, the New Zealand Shipping Co's agents wrote asking whether the port could accommodate the *Rakaia* on her next visit. The *Rakaia* was eight years old, 5629 tons gross and 128 metres long. Ramsay explained that although she could enter port, she would vulnerable if a nor-westerly gale caught her alongside the wharf, since there was no good holding ground for anchors. The board optimistically (to be charitable) told the shipping agent to bring in the *Rakaia*, but the firm's principals wisely diverted her.

It was now plain that unless improvements were made, more ships would bypass Oamaru, further reducing revenue. Late in 1903, therefore, the board's standing committee examined its options. Previous studies had projected Sumpter-style wharves from the mole or from the southern edge of the harbour, but the choice now lay between improving Sumpter Wharf and building a large wharf along the mole itself. Sumpter Wharf could be improved for £4000, but extending it would eat into the swinging basin (where ships were turned) and leave the port short of space at busy times, since Macandrew Wharf

It took time to finalise access arrangements to the new wharf. A Wansbeck Street alignment offered the most direct access, but the Railway Department insisted on what the Otago Witness *called 'a devious and most unsatisfactory approach from Itchen Street' from near the grain elevator. In April 1907, the harbour board decided to run a road along the foreshore north from where Waterfront Road. That was fine for goods, but not for pedestrians, who demanded an overhead footbridge to shave a kilometre off the trek from town. Here it awaited restoration in 2007. The old grain silos in the background were removed in February 2008.* – Gavin McLean

(redecked in 1889) and the Cross Wharf were now rarely used. A new wharf on the mole would, with associated dredging, cost £10,000, but it would leave Sumpter free for use by other ships. After the receiver and ratepayers okayed the project, tenders were let and Fitzgerald & Bignell started work in 1906.

By April 1907 the Railways Department had certified the sidings on the new wharf, now known as Holmes Wharf, named after chairman James Holmes. The honour of officially opening it went to Shaw Savill & Albion's freighter *Waiwera*. Distinctive for her unusually tall funnel, she was 6237 tons gross and 129.8 metres long. Looking forward to 'the beginning of a new and prosperous epoch in the history of the local Harbour Board and in the commercial life of Oamaru', the town welcomed her heartily.

She arrived on the night of 6 June and anchored in the roadstead to await daylight. Next morning Captain Ramsay went out and decided to take her in at the peak of high tide, when there would be 9.1 metres of water alongside the berth. At midday, a large crowd on Holmes Wharf gave three cheers as Ramsay put the *Waiwera* alongside without a hitch. Board members, local politicians and businessmen streamed up the gangway to inspect the ship and at 1430 treated the ships' officers to a speech-filled luncheon at the Star & Garter Hotel in Itchen Street.

'It is now four years since the last oversea vessel was berthed at the Oamaru Wharf', the *Oamaru Mail* stated erroneously, recalling the trouble-plagued 25 June 1903 visit by the *Maori*. This time everything went smoothly. The watersiders started loading at 1400 hours on Friday 7 June, and after pausing for an evening meal break, worked until 0100 hours the following day, loading 11,000 carcasses. By the time loading finished on Saturday, the *Waiwera* had loaded 20,819 carcasses of mutton, 866 legs and pieces, 82 casks of tallow and 260 bales of wool. That

was twice the number of carcasses shipped through the port the previous year. Harbour board officials talked confidently about shipping at least 80,000 of the 106,000 sheep killed at the freezing works. Storekeepers looked forward to more visits by more of the twenty Home boats previously unable to enter port. That weekend butcher J. Gilchrist had displayed 170 poultry heads to show the size of the order he had received from the *Waiwera*, and 'John Chinaman's share of the deal was £5 for vegetables.'[32]

Weeks later, the *Rakaia* followed the *Waiwera*. It will be remembered that this ship bypassed the port after her agents learned of Ramsay's length restriction on ships using Sumpter Wharf. The board gave her a *Waiwera*-style welcome. Members gathered on the wharf, but she was late and by the time she turned up, the seas had made it too dangerous to enter. So, after bouncing around in the roadstead uncomfortably for four hours, the *Rakaia* left for Port Chalmers. She returned to Oamaru later that week.

The incident was shrugged off, because board members were still laughing at their Timaru rivals. Weeks earlier the Timaru Harbour Board released a fancy, carefully-composed photograph of its port. The photographer lovingly captured the new wharves, sheds and other recent improvements, all topped off by an impressive forest of masts and funnels. Timaru triumphant! The board sent copies to the illustrated weekly papers, who printed the picture, two mislabelling it 'Oamaru'. Oamaruvians roared with laughter when told that the Timaru chairman asked an Oamaru rival how much they had paid the press to steal their thunder!

Oamaru's greatest maritime
moment? Taken from the
foreshore, this photograph
shows the Waiwera *towering
over Holmes Wharf on the
narrow north mole. The*
Progress *lies in the swinging
basin, while Sumpter Wharf
is busy with a freighter on
either side.*

– North Otago Museum

Chapter Four

'FISHING FOR COD WITH GOLDFISH'?
1907–1940

It made damning reading. In May 1908, as Oamaru Harbour Board members, still under the thumb of the receiver, squabbled and bickered over borrowing money to build a new dredge, the *Otago Witness* served up a potted history of this potty port. 'The Oamaru Harbour Board, since it came into existence 30 odd years ago, has borrowed £317,000, in seven sums ranging from £100,000 to £10,000', it wrote.

Of this money £160,000 was raised in London the balance was subscribed in the colonies. According to the board's balance sheets, every penny has been spent, directly and indirectly, in constructing and improving the port of Oamaru. It has served to build a breakwater, one large and three or four small wharves, to purchase a dredge that is now, it is stated, owing to corrosion and other causes, refused a certificate by the Marine Department to dig two enormous holes in the side of Cape Wanbrow, to buy a big steam crane that now lies desolately rusting at the end of the breakwater, to build a wall of rocks around the foreshore, and to carry out a multitude of small and necessary works. It is said that borrowed wealth has served to make a number of building contractors glad and rich …

From this it may be gathered that Oamaru's artificial harbour has not, as yet, proved itself a source of large revenue and profits and surpluses and other joy-producing things. Within the last few years the coastal ships calling at the port have steadily increased in numbers and in size, and during the past 12 months the *Waiwera*, *Rakaia*, *Aotea*, and *Papanui* have loaded cargo direct for London from the new Holmes wharf; but this slight activity is scarcely what one would look for after the expenditure of a third of a million of money.

Many years ago, apparently, certain men in Oamaru had a vision. Snuggled in around the corner formed by Cape Wanbrow and the East Coast they saw a great city; behind it, and to the south and north, miles and miles of fertile rolling plains stretched away, whereon grew wheat and oats and potatoes, sheep and cattle, in great confusion. All round they saw the vomiting smoke stacks of countless factories, and, cosily berthed behind a big breakwater, many inter-ocean steamers, filling capacious holds with the produce of North Otago. It was a pleasing picture, and the men who saw asked 'Why Not?' So they told what they had seen to the ratepayers and the ratepayers agreed that it was good, and that the

Diver James Lake suits up on the dredge Progress *alongside Sumpter Wharf. The small sheds (left, background) still survive. The large one to the right, which burned down in the 1970s, was for many years the Oamaru base for Port Chalmers stevedore and shipping agent John Mill & Co; it also housed a wool dumping plant. – J.M. Forrester album, North Otago Museum 6709*

port should be got ready for that fleet of ocean-going steamers. The necessary money was borrowed, and, as already stated, the breakwater and wharves built. But, in the meantime, right along the back of the district the Government built the Otago Central railway, which came direct from Dunedin; to the north, Timaru (which is the only port between Oamaru and Lyttelton) built a breakwater and wharves, and bought a dredge, and made a safe anchorage for big ships—and Timaru is the centre of a district that stretches from Glenavy to Ashburton, and that does not support a railway running at the back of it. It is said that Timaru, building its breakwater at a later period than did Oamaru, profited by the mistakes made by the latter town, and constructed a better and cheaper port. Timaru has already proved a successful port. This has all served to limit the potentialities of Oamaru's harbour; and then there is the preferential railway tariff. It costs 25s to send a ton of ordinary goods from Palmerston to Dunedin by rail; the same quantity can be railed from Oamaru to Dunedin (or vice versa) for 12s 6d ...

All this told against the Oamaru port: up till very recently only coastal steamers called, and, as the cost of transhipment of overseas cargo was greater than railing it to Port Chalmers ... After the completion of the breakwater, the rubble protecting wall and the small wharf known as Sumpter's, the board for a long time contented itself with dredging, deepening the entrance and the basin. Two or three small steamers per week was the average, and once or twice a big vessel, tempted with a cargo direct for Europe, ventured in. But for these vessels the port was shallow, the wharf accommodation not nearly sufficient, and the entrance awkward, and shipping companies did not show any eagerness in sending their big boats to Oamaru. So about 1903 the board bestirred itself, and borrowed another £17,000, with which Holmes Wharf was built This, then was the position a year ago, when the board declared the Holmes wharf completed, and the port ready to receive boats of the *Waiwera* class. The Christchurch Meat Company got ready a cargo of frozen meat, from its Oamaru works, and shortly afterwards the *Waiwera* was brought safely into the port of Oamaru. Oamaru took a holiday, and declared itself very proud and glad, and while many thousands of frozen sheeps' carcasses were hustled into the holds of the big

steamer, Oamaru's public men assembled en masse and feted the *Waiwera*'s officers. The *Waiwera*'s officers made speeches, and said that the port of Oamaru was quite as good and safe as the port of Timaru—and Oamaru, hearing this, exulted openly. The big rates, and the loan default were forgotten, and 'a new era of prosperity' was foreshadowed, and when the *Waiwera*'s officers said that the basin might advantageously be deepened, Oamaru declared 'we will dredge!' When the *Waiwera* went away, the board sat often and secretly in solemn conclave, and the uninitiated were told that it discussed dredging. Meanwhile the *Rakaia* arrived and took away frozen meat, and her officers were also feted. And, at regular intervals after that came the *Aotea* and the *Papanui*, each loading up with frozen meat and produce for Home markets. These steamers came in without mishap, and left again unscathed, but the officers of each talking with harbour board members and officials 'plumped' for deeper water. The board found itself in a quandary.

... the district now tapped by Oamaru port is now limited. Timaru is progressing by leaps and bounds, and practically the whole of the produce of the country north of Morven goes to that town. The extension of the Otago Central railway to Omakau, via Naseby district, has diverted to Dunedin the whole of the produce of that district. Had that line come down from the Central, via Naseby to Oamaru, it is reasonable to suppose that those London bondholders would not now be paying £500 per annum for the services of a receiver ... Was it worth while, in view of the obvious limitations of the district, to favour the borrowing of a large sum to be expended in the further dredging and deepening of the port, or would it be of greater advantage financially merely to devote a greater sum to the maintenance of the harbour as is?

It was a fair question. The reporter's prose may have been purpler than a cardinal's robes, but he was right about those cosy (and costly) little chats with Home boat skippers. In all the speechifying at the reception for the *Waiwera*, one aside by the chairman stood out: 'What we want, Captain, is a first class dredge, and plenty of money.'

Dredging is the hidden asset in any port. Wharves, cranes, tugs and dredges are obvious; expensively dredged

shipping channels and swinging basins are not. Yet everything depends on digging the channels deep and keeping them that way. Without deep water, ships will not call. Ships can wait for high water, but owners grumble about the cost of delays and will go elsewhere if they can. 'Time is money', Shaw Savill's local superintendent complained about the *Waiwera* having to wait half a day to catch the tide.

Try as they might, however, the chairman and harbourmaster failed to get their modern dredge. In 1907–08 the board divided into two nearly evenly-balanced camps. Some wanted a new dredge. Others wanted to renovate the *Progress* to handle routine maintenance, hiring bigger dredges for occasional port deepening – good financial discipline, they argued. At stake was the difference between spending £50,000 or £15,000, but the quality of the debate was not helped by doubts about the condition of the *Progress*. She had been designed for an earlier generation of ships. Was she worth rebuilding? No one seemed to know. In 1907 Dunedin engineer Alexander Morrison dismissed enlarging her hopper as 'unpracticable'. She needed a new boiler and tail-shaft, repairs to her deck, and new anchors and cables to handle the increased boiler power, £5750 in all.[1] A few months later another consultant, McIntyre, said otherwise, so the board asked the Marine Department's machinery inspector for a third opinion. Bureaucratic constipation by consulting is nothing new.

In 1908, the board voted narrowly to borrow £50,000 to buy a new dredge and to deepen the port, a bare majority accepting that it would take £30,000 and eight years for the rebuilt *Progress* to do what a new ship would do in three.[2] Board member W.H. Rose, Shaw Savill's local representative, led the opposition, supported by John Reid, Donald Borrie, Jasper Nicholls and R.W. Monson. Initially supportive, Rose, like Monson, the Union Company local manager, calculated that the revenue from one or two Home boats a month would never repay the investment: 'fishing for cod with goldfish', he called it.[3] Rose knew that ships' water, a larger swinging basin and a modern dredge – it was only natural – 'but what is the wisdom of dredging to 20ft when the bed of the ocean outside is about 17ft? … Isn't it to buy a machine to do what is called about two years' work, and then ratepayers are to have the satisfaction of seeing her gradually deteriorating in the harbour, costing them a pretty penny for upkeep, insurance, interest, and the sinking fund until the loan runs out.'

Others disagreed, passionately. Things grew so acrimonious that Chairman Robert Milligan told Rose and Borrie to resign, then he challenged Rose to contest an election against him. Parliament passed the Oamaru Harbour Board Loan Act 1908, but ratepayers, probably sick of the board's bickering, torpedoed its plans at the poll. Rose was hero of the day. In November 1909 seventy supporters honoured him for 'championing the small dredge'. They reimbursed his legal expenses and donated 'an illuminated address, a gold sovereign case, and an inscribed gold pendant'.

A hundred years ago sailing ships rarely visited Oamaru, which was well served by the Union Company's sophisticated east coast South Island 'main trunk' route. A rare exception was the 860-ton barque Lobo, *which brought Tasmanian timber in March 1914. The curve of the white railings in the background shows the narrow width of the mole before its 1966–71 reconstruction. Note, too, the raised rail lines. Some were made flush with the decking in the 1930s and the remainder were modified in the 1960s. – North Otago Museum 1899*

OAMARU – A SIGHTSEERS' DESTINATION

Every year, for several decades, the Union Steam Ship Company ran Boxing Day and New Year's Day excursions, often bringing 1000 holidaymakers into town.

This is a report of the Tarawera's *excursion on New Year's Day 1908.*

The s.s. *Tarawera* carried a full complement of excursionists to Oamaru on New Year's Day, about 1100 making the trip, and the popularity of the excursion is shown by the fact that many had the misfortune to be left behind. Within 15 minutes of the time appointed for her departure the *Tarawera* cast off, and those on board settled down to enjoy the lovely panoramic view of Dunedin and the harbour. Once outside the Heads it was seen that a calm trip was in store for the excursionists, and as the atmospheric conditions were favourable, glasses and binoculars were in frequent use spying out the familiar landmarks. The 'McKenzie' Cairn could be seen standing out in bold against the sky. This and the usual fun and merry-making, together with music by the band, passed the time very pleasantly, till the vessel's arrival at the White City. Many of the residents were congregated on the new wharf, expecting the boat to be berthed there; but this was not to be, and they had perforce to walk a fairly long distance to the old jetty. It would have perhaps, suited the excursionists better if the boat

Hundreds – look at the bicycles in the foreground – turned out to greet 800 New Year's Day excursionists from Dunedin when the Moura *berthed at Sumpter Wharf on 1 January 1902. The passengers had danced to the music of a 'German band' on the way up the coast, and Captain Beaumont had reassured the nervous that his course took him two miles clear of the recent wreck of the* Antiocco Accame *off Danger Reef. The ship berthed at 12.30, allowing passengers to catch the sports competitions. The return trip was rougher, exacerbated by the legendary rolling abilities of the* Moura *(2027 tons, 1899), a narrow, shallow-draft ship built to serve the small port of Strahan, Tasmania. As it was too rough to dance, passengers conducted a political debate over Dunedin parliamentarian Alfred Barclay, which culminated in the crowd singing 'We'll hang old Barclay on a sour apple tree.' – North Otago Museum 296*

had berthed at the new wharf, as they would then have had less distance to travel to town. The two hours' spell in Oamaru was mainly spent satisfying the inner man and strolling round the town and through the beautiful gardens, where everything was in tip-top order. By 3.30 all the excursionists re-embarked for the return journey, which all concerned declared to be as enjoyable as the outward one. At times the *Tarawera* was playing at pitch and toss, but the amount of seasickness was comparatively small. Shortly after leaving Oamaru the excursionists were treated to the unusual opportunity of seeing a man go up in a balloon and descend gently to *terra firma* with the aid of a parachute. This turned out to be the balloon sent up from the local sports ground. Dunedin was reached shortly before 9 o'clock, everyone appearing pleased with the day's outing. Praise is due to the captain, officers, and those concerned in the running of the boat. No accident of any kind occurred to mar the pleasure of the trip.[4]

The Tarawera *(2007 tons, 1882) conducted the Union Company's Oamaru excursions from 1905 to 1908. 'Quago' covered the 1907 excursion for the 'Dot's Little Folk' children's page in the* Otago Witness. *The twenty-five DLF from Dunedin were met by their Oamaru counterparts and led a short distance to the park where a picnic had been laid on. There romance bloomed. 'One blushing young lad who, on the outward trip, sang "No girl can have this coon", would give us nothing but "I'M in love with Mary"', 'Quago' reported. 'After he had finished he sat in a corner by himself, no doubt picturing in his mind Mary, whom he had left behind.' This is probably the 1906 excursion. Note that a start has been made on building Holmes Wharf on the mole. – North Otago Museum 983*

Rose's victory was pyrrhic. The board, of which he was a member, had lost money and mana over the issue and the pain was not over yet. The receiver returned its account for poll expenses of £350 and said that he would not pay up unless ordered to by the court. A judge duly sanctioned the expenditure, but the evidence made embarrassing reading. Milligan admitted that the board's deep divisions and need for so many meetings had cost dearly 'for motor cars and for locomotion expenses'.[5] Then the poll itself was struck down. In February 1909 T. Hutchinson S.M. found for complainants and declared it void. In theory the board might have gone for another poll, but common sense finally prevailed. It was time to lick wounds and rebuild internal unity.

But that still left the question what they should do with the *Progress*. In 1910, after much debate, the board accepted the advice of yet more consultants, W.H. Paterson and J. Blair, to convert her to a stationary dredge. She would end her days filling pontoons and pipelines reclaiming the western edge of the harbour for industrial land. She returned from Stephenson & Cook's Port Chalmers shipyard in January 1911 to work for contractor J. Lothian. The *Progress* spent a further six years at Oamaru before undergoing an unlikely resurrection: conversion into a sailing ship to meet wartime demand for shipping. In the 1920s she traded to Oamaru (after another reconstruction) and lasted until wrecked in Cook Strait in 1931.

The *Progress* was not the only thing wearing out. The generation that had built the harbour works was dying or retiring. Captain William Sewell had retired as harbourmaster in 1896. His successor, Captain James Ramsay, served until 1922. In March 1907, Thomas Forrester, best remembered for the buildings he designed in partnership with John Lemon, died after a short illness. He had started with the dock trust in the early 1870s and had superintended the port's engineering projects, right up to preparing the plans for Holmes Wharf: 'The wharf, now completed, is regarded as one of the best constructed in the colony', his obituary observed.[6] Forrester's successor, G.A.K. Darbyshire, attended one board meeting, contracted pneumonia and died in August. His replacement, C.A. La Roche, made of tougher stuff, went on to serve until 1930. In 1911, Frank Peach retired as board accountant. He had joined the harbour board a year after it was formed.

One of Peach's nightmares had been the board's debts, which had piled up faster than shingle off the breakwater tip. As we saw, it had stopped paying interest on its 1879 loan and had been accruing debt at the rate of over £6000 on this loan alone. This had been humiliating. Almost every payment had to be approved by the receiver and the bondholders objected to even modest development work.

In December 1896, for example, Justice Williams had authorised spending £12,800 just to keep the harbour operating. The 1879 debenture bondholders objected, but the judge ruled that the work (mainly dredging) would make a profit. Even so, the bondholders of 1876 and 1879 were still out of pocket, owed £34,500 and £102,000 in overdue interest respectively. In 1899, the same judge ordered the board to establish a sinking fund to set aside £800 annually.

By 1908 the board had worn down the bondholders and persuaded them to accept £47,000 in full settlement of the £102,000 owed. The Oamaru Harbour Board Enabling Act dismayed the *Evening Post*, which condemned 'the practice of disguising a Loan Bill under the title of an "Aid to Public Works and Land Settlement Bill"' to 'deal with the disastrous results of injudicious borrowing', but it gave the board a fresh start.[7]

World War I was a severe trial. The statistics made depressing reading. Overseas shipping virtually dried up and was confined to a handful of trans-Tasman ships, as vessels were requisitioned for wartime service or sunk by U-boats. The tonnage of coastal ships entering port also declined, from a peak of 181,091 tons in 1912 to 89,780

Damage to the glass plate surreally frames this portrait of a perfect Edwardian day at Friendly Bay. Children paddle, women parade with parasols and the band plays, while a Home boat loads at Holmes Wharf in the background.

– North Otago Museum 4265

tons in 1917 and 69,617 tons in 1918. It recovered slightly to 91,617 tons in 1919, before sliding another 13,000 tons in 1920.

The wartime coastal arrivals and departures had a sameness about them, just a few regular callers running a reduced service. Most were Union Company vessels – the *Corinna*, *Kahika*, *Poerua* etc – but the Holm Shipping Company's *John* was there, as was the little steamer *Kotare*, bringing timber from Southland. Some transhipped cargo that might formerly have left port in a Home boat, but great quantities of wool, meat and skins were simply railed to Timaru or Port Chalmers. The only new cargo was 'cases of good cheer' for 'the boys of North Otago at the front', shipped free by the Union Company. The shipping service was bare-bones, though. In November 1915, for example, just fifteen ships entered port and late that month the *Oamaru Mail* advised shippers that the *Wanaka*, due from Auckland in early December, would be

their last opportunity to ship to the country's major city before the New Year.

Shipping took some time to return to normal. The coastal fleet got back to business quickly enough, but for several years a general shortage of shipping kept the overseas ships away from Oamaru. After the harbour board lobbied the Overseas Shipowners' Allotment Committee (OSAC), which represented the Conference Lines, Home boats returned to Oamaru in 1921, when the *Karamea* and the *Waimate* arrived to load. More followed, with the visit of the 7463-ton new motor ship *Port Dunedin* in September 1926 being a highlight. The return of overseas ships also brought a small but welcome injection of new faces into

OAMARU MAKES HISTORY
– THE *TERRA NOVA*

'And so at 2.30 A.M. on 10 February we crept like a phantom ship into the little harbour of Oamaru on the east coast of New Zealand. With what mixed feelings we smelt the old familiar woods and grassy slopes, and saw the shadowy outlines of human homes. With untiring persistence the little lighthouse blinked out the message, "What ship's that?" "What ship's that?" They were obviously puzzled and disturbed at getting no answer. A boat was lowered and Pennell and Atkinson were rowed ashore and landed. The seamen had orders to answer no questions. After a little the boat returned, and Crean announced: "We was chased, sorr, but they got nothing out of us. We put out to sea."'

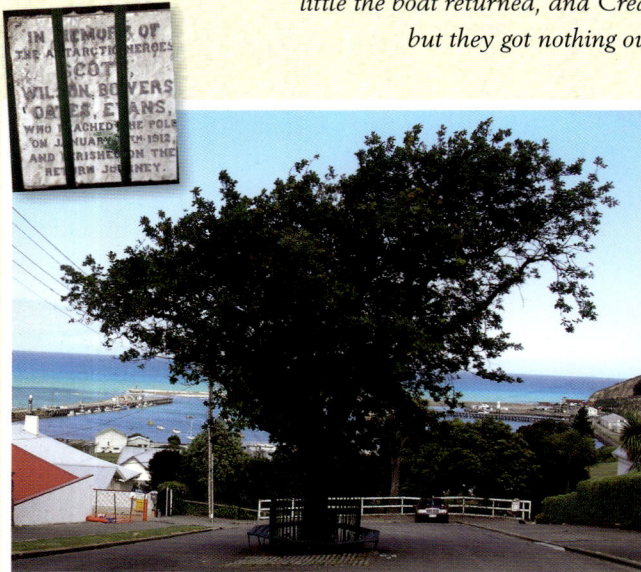

That account comes from *Worst Journey in the World*, a classic of adventure writing. Author Apsley Cherry-Garrard had crewed aboard the *Terra Nova* with Robert Falcon Scott's 1910–13 expedition and was looking longingly at Oamaru, the first 'normal' landscape he had seen in three years.

He was wrong in one small detail. The inquiring 'lighthouse' was merely the Oamaru Harbour Board's night watchman. In the dark early hours of the morning, Neil McKinnon saw the lights of a ship appear off the breakwater. Thinking her the *Ngatoro*, which was expected that day, he signalled her to stand off because it was low tide. She complied, but signalled that she was sending a boat ashore.

This was unusual. So when McKinnon saw a dinghy rowed by four men, he signalled it to come alongside Sumpter Wharf. The boat's occupants did this, but ignored requests to divulge the name of their ship. When he directed his lantern onto the boat, they said he was wasting his time looking for a name on it.

McKinnon was now very suspicious. He had repeatedly demanded to know their identity and had even threatened to call the police, but the strangers had merely replied that he could bring 'the police, the customs officer, the harbourmaster or anybody else he jolly well liked; he was going to get no information out of them.' At this point, two men got out of the dinghy, which the other pair rowed back to the ship, barely visible just beyond the breakwater in the dark.

Who was the port's mysterious visitor? The argument continued as they walked back to the night watchman's hut until, learning that the harbourmaster, Captain Ramsay, could be telephoned, the men asked McKinnon to summon him. The penny seems to have finally dropped; observing the strangers' appearance and garb, McKinnon commented that 'You've come from further south than the Bluff.'

He directed them to Ramsay's house, though the harbourmaster walked down Arun Street to escort them up the hill to his residence, where they slept on the drawing room floor. They identified themselves as Lieutenant Harry Pennell and Surgeon Edward Atkinson of the *Terra Nova*. Apparently, too, the men swore Ramsay and port medical officer Dr Alexander Douglas to secrecy. 'Owing to press contracts and the necessity of preventing leakage of news the *Terra Nova* had to remain at sea for twenty-four hours after a cable had been sent to England', Cherry-Garrard continued. 'Also it was of the first importance that the relatives should be informed of the facts before the newspapers published them.'

So the secrecy continued after daylight. At the start of business on Monday morning a coded message was sent to London via Christchurch advising of the deaths in March 1912 of Captain Robert Falcon Scott, Edward Wilson, 'Birdie' Bowers, L. E. Oates and Edward Evans. John Meehan, the telegraphist on duty, was then detained for a period on his own to 'avoid speculation'. Captain Ramsay had meanwhile bought railway tickets for Pennell and Atkinson, who departed Oamaru's station incognito for Christchurch to meet the *Terra Nova*, which arrived at Lyttelton the next day with flags flying at half-mast, having spent time cruising off the coast trying to avoid detection by coastal steamers.

The news rocked the world and within four hours of sending the telegram from Oamaru, crowds were forming in London to honour a British hero.

Oamaru never forgot its footnote in world history. Before the year was out a memorial oak tree had been planted in Arun Street, complete with wrought iron fence and marble plaque honouring 'the Antarctic Heroes, Scott, Wilson, Bowers, Oates and Evans, who reached the South Pole on January 18th 1912 and perished on the return journey.'

Photos – Gavin McLean

the community. The ships were freighters, not passenger liners, but British cargo vessels were not obliged to employ a doctor if they carried twelve passengers or fewer, so many offered a few berths to travellers who preferred the leisurely pace of freighter travel. In September 1923, for example, when the *Paparoa* berthed, the *Oamaru Mail*'s social column reported the arrival of the passengers Mr W. Sutherland, Miss E. McLeod, Mr and Mrs Robert Stannes and a Richard Stannes. McLeod and the Stannes were from Scotland and the Stannes intended to settle in the district.

Losing the wartime overseas trade must have jolted the board, because it wooed OSAC assiduously. The chairman's 1926 annual report thanked the committee for its improved co-operation during the year, noting an increase in exports of 30,000 carcasses and 300 more bales of wool over the previous season. By 1927, this partnership ensured that the port was now 'shipping the whole of the meat frozen in the district' and that the lines were asking about the port's ability to accommodate a *Matakana*-class ship. Although the old wool clippers and the converted sailing ships had often sailed from Oamaru for London direct, it had been a long time since a ship had made Oamaru its first port of call. In 1928, however, board members Edward Lane and Robert Milligan met the

The Home boat Kaikoura *at Holmes Wharf in 1922, with the port's fishing fleet in the foreground. Little is known about fishing at Oamaru, where fish hawking was a very low rung on the Victorian economic ladder. W. Smith established a fish-freezing works in 1895, and by 1907 most boats were oil engine craft. In July 1906 the* Oamaru Mail *reported that Dunedin boat builder J. McPherson had delivered a new 9.1-metre, kauri-hull boat to Oamaru fishmonger A.F. Cross. It made eight miles per hour with its Standard oil engine, but also carried sails. A year later the occupants of another launch were attacked by a seven-metre shark eight or nine miles off the port. They later found large teeth marks on the boat's keel.*
– Gavin McLean Collection

A ship's officer supervises the lightly-laden Kaikoura's *departure. The 6998-ton four-master had been built in 1903.*
— *North Otago Museum 4034*

lines in London and persuaded them to trial an inward direct voyage. The *Rimutaka* docked at Holmes Wharf in April 1929 direct, with 882 tons of cargo. The *Raranaga* followed later that year, followed by the *Rimutaka* and the *Turakina* in 1930 and the *Port Hunter* in 1931. Machinery and steel for the Waitaki hydro dam helped the early shipments, which averaged between 1250–1500 tonnes of imports. In 1930, the board fitted electric capstans and bollards to Holmes Wharf to improve the handling of these ships. Throughout the 1930s, one or two ships

called direct from London in addition to the many vessels which loaded lamb and wool for exports. Oamaru people grew accustomed to the sight of bigger and bigger Home boats.

The port was now at the limit of its capacity. In 1932 the average depth at the entrance was 6.4 metres at low water; at Holmes Wharf there was 7.9 metres, while Sumpter Wharf had 6.7 metres at low water at the east side and 5.8–6.7 metres on the west side. Things had never been better. But while the 1930s would see two ships of

The coaster Holmdale *heads for Sumpter Wharf, where the Timaru dredge 350 is moored. The big freighter at Holmes Wharf is the Federal Steam Navigation Co's* Westmoreland *(9512 tons, 1917), a four-master like many early Federal ships. She is riding high, since the lines sent their bigger ships to Oamaru lightly-laden. – North Otago Museum 2550*

A flivver delivered. Until the early 1970s, vehicles were carried as deck cargo. Oamaru's car salesmen remember going down to collect the vehicles, which then needed plenty of 'elbow grease' to remove their protective coating of grease for the sea voyage. This Model A coupe is being unloaded on Holmes Wharf in 1929. – North Otago Museum 4219

more than 10,000 tons load at Oamaru – the New Zealand Shipping Co's *Opawa* (10,107 tons) and *Otaio* (10,048 tons) – draft limitations caused the diversion of three ships in 1931–2 and several callers to adjust their schedules to load at Oamaru while still lightly laden. It was time to think about radical solutions.

The challenge was to dredge a channel to deeper water. In 1914, the board had commissioned Lyttelton engineer Cyrus Williams to report on improving the harbour. Williams outlined the fundamental problems:

(1) the alignment of the breakwater ruled out extending it into substantially deeper water and (2) the seabed was too compact to be dredged in the open sea. To achieve worthwhile improvements, the board would have to dredge a 76-metre wide channel under shelter and match Timaru's depths, 5.8 metres at low water and 8.3 metres at high water.

Williams's solution, influenced by Timaru's breakwater extension, was to build a 533-metre breakwater extension to the 5.8-metre mark at an angle of 40 degrees east of true north. The extension, starting 170 metres from the outer end of the breakwater, would require 250,000 tonnes of rock. Williams would have liked to have used the board's quarry, but after learning that 75 per cent of the rock used for the mole had been rejected, he recommended railing stone from Port Chalmers. This would go in the top work, where larger rocks had to take the force of the sea. Ironically, the Railway Department's predatory pricing made getting stone from Port Chalmers relatively cheap.

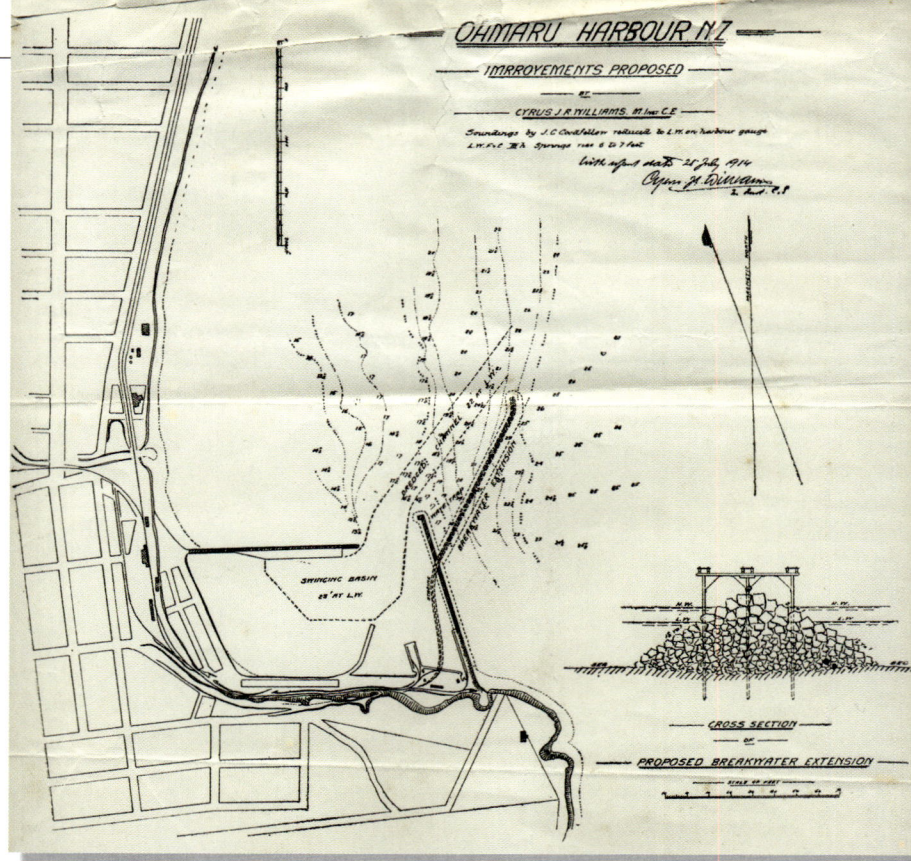

*Cyrus Williams's 1913
plan featured a breakwater
extension angled out to
provide a sheltered shipping
channel.* –Gavin McLean

With a small hopper grab dredge fitted with a trailing sand suction pump thrown in, the bill would be £123,153 if a £20,883 concession on the railage from Port Chalmers was negotiated.[8]

The harbour board of 1914 did not have that kind of money, but twenty years later its finances were more shipshape. The diversion of three ships in 1931 and the brief grounding of the *Kent* on the evening of 29 July 1933 caused board members to think again. In 1933 they commissioned F.W. Furkert to suggest a solution. His report bore certain similarities to Williams's. While acknowledging that the breakwater 'has been a highly satisfactory work', he found some faults. Because the blocks were of the same size, they did not 'break joint' as they should and did not interlock, adding extra strength.[9] Because the joint between the extension and the existing structure would concentrate the force of the waves and throw them higher, he recommended raising the old structure to prevent waves overtopping it and carrying debris into the harbour, thereby reducing ongoing dredging costs. Furkert's 268-metre long extension would go out to the 6.7-metre mark; future extensions would continue at right angles to the original breakwater. It would also reduce or eliminate sand and shingle build-up around the breakwater tip, further reducing dredging costs. The old tip would become a wave trap.

The total cost would be £96,000. While acknowledging the board's desire to construct the works from quarry rock and, in view of high unemployment, to use as much unskilled and semiskilled labour as possible, Furkert was cautious. His trawl through the files showed that, during the mole's construction, board members had complained about the lengthy and costly delays caused by the high proportion of small stone and waste rock. John McGregor had been worried enough to cast a few small concrete blocks as an alternative, but had to stick with the quarry after the contractor 'made what Mr McGregor considered exorbitant demands'. Furkert noted that 'I have been advised that it is a tradition in the town that the contractors, while not making any great profit out of their rock work, were doing very well at the price which the Board paid them for the rubbish and spoil from the quarry which was used for reclamation purposes.'[10] He recommended seeking prices for concrete, quarry stone or a mix of quarry rock and harder stone from Timaru or Port Chalmers.

The prospect of using at least some of the cheap quarry rock seems to have mesmerised board members, who were further seduced by the Nobel Explosive Co's salesman, who professed himself amazed to find 'a marine work so well endowed with a quarry so close to its work, and with such a good quality of stone suitable for marine work.'[11] The stone was not, but a trial shot was fired on 8 June 1934,

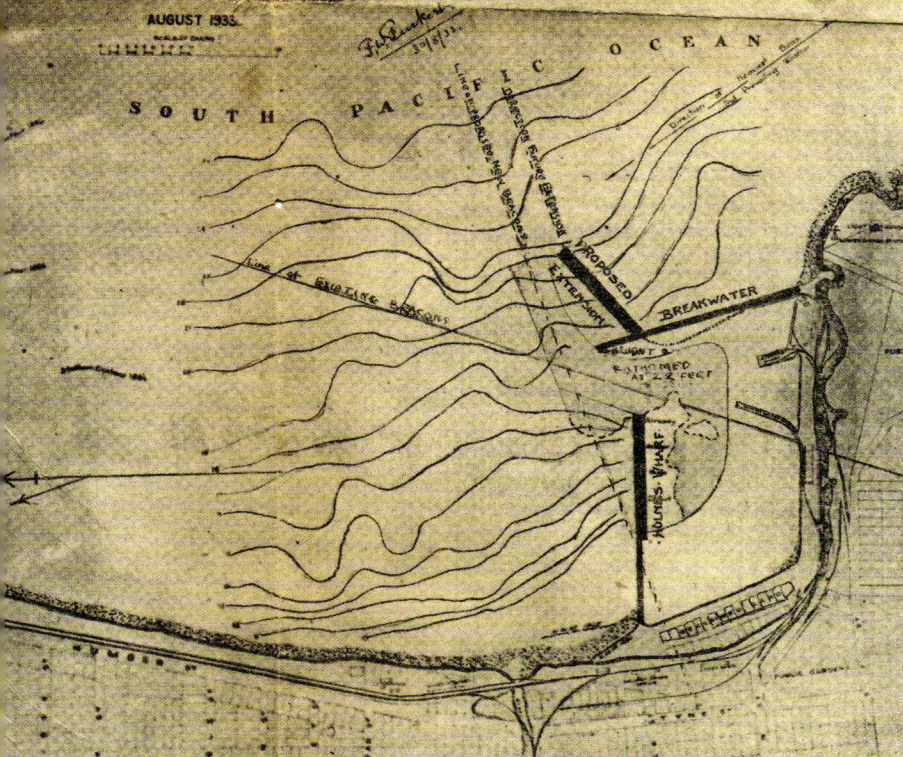

OAMARU HARBOUR.
SHOWING BREAKWATER EXTENSION & DREDGING
AS PROPOSED BY F.W.FURKERT. M.I.C.E.
AUGUST 1933.

Furkert's 1933 was a reduced-scale variation on Cyrus Williams's earlier plan. – Oamaru Mail

and was declared highly successful. On 7 November 1935 a second shot brought down 40,000 tonnes of rock, and more blasts followed, including one disastrous one on 16 August 1938 when 150,000 tonnes of rock rained down on to the board's blacksmith's and engine sheds. By then, too, the board's consulting engineer, G.A. Lee of Auckland, had provoked warnings from Furkert about Lee increasing the length of the extension by 37 metres and beginning it about 100 metres from the outer end.

Obsessed by a few ship diversions, and keen to tap into government-subsidised labour, the board decided to build the first 152-metre length with rock from its quarry.

This would cost £27,000 and, helped by a £4000 subsidy from the Unemployment Board, would leave money in the £33,000 improvements and renewals fund. In July 1934 it endorsed the scheme, unwittingly overturning one of Furkert's safeguards, independent analysis from competing tenderers about the rock's durability.

Second-hand equipment was purchased, empowering legislation was passed by Parliament and work got under way in 1936. Progress was slow, frequently hindered by heavy seas, and in 1938–9 the extension – named the Ramsay Extension – grew just seven metres. By 1940, it was only 62.5 metres long.

Waterfronts are about more than ships and cargo, of course. People walked the wharves and fished from them.

Wasted effort? Officials walk the breakwater while workers tip another load of quarry rock on to the Ramsay Extension. The harbour board bought the locomotive in 1934.
– North Otago Museum 2599

Newspaper reports in the 1890s and the early 1900s mentioned quinnat salmon and trout being taken by trevalli fishermen – in December 1900 four 'fine trout' were killed when the harbour board blasted a rock off Normanby Wharf. There were also occasional reports of seals swimming off the Cross Wharf and of sharks being sighted in the harbour. In April 1900, the Todd brothers caught a shark 'fully 7 feet long' in their net in the harbour.

George Bowden's clinker-built launch Lily *leads another boat past the breakwater.* – North Otago Museum 279

Some swimmers took the waters between the Cross Wharf and Normanby Wharf, near the old slipway. By World War I attention had mostly switched to the other side of the harbour, where sand accumulating at the western end of Holmes Wharf provided a pleasant pocket beach. In 1921, the friendly societies' picnic committee sponsored the emergence of the Foreshore Improvements Committee, which the council and the harbour board backed. The timing was right. In the period between 1922 and 1929 the board tidied up the reclamation, leasing tank storage land to the oil companies and working with the borough and the improvements committee on roading, fencing and beautifying the area.

In 1922, a 'queen carnival' (a beauty contest) raised money by inviting people to name the beach for a penny a vote: Friendly Bay was the winner. Over the years

the Friendly Bay Improvement Society landscaped the area, adding a bathing pavilion, tea kiosk, band rotunda, children's playground and an art deco esplanade.

So Oamaruvians took to the water. The Oamaru Boating Club's shells and skiffs powered across the harbour, and from 1937 the sea scouts were revived as Scott's Own Sea Scouts. In fine weather, less energetic townsfolk paddled and swam in their safe little pocket of the Pacific. But was it? Probably not. In 1923 an *Oamaru Mail* reporter made an unpleasant discovery when reporting the work of the dredge *Canterbury*, which was clanking and thumping away impressively, biting 100 tonnes a minute from the shingle bank that had built up between the breakwater and Sumpter Wharf. When she moved closer to Holmes Wharf, 'one sniff was enough as a thick, black, slimy, greasy ooze with a green frothy scum above it poured into the hopper

Improvement
Society marker.
– Gavin McLean

*A crowd assembles on the
Cross Wharf to admire the
new motor launch* Leader,
*built by George Boaden, Joe
Martyn and Jim Williams.
The tin shed leaning over
the wharf's edge in this early
1930s photograph is an old
'thunder box', unhealthily
close to the Surf Bay bathing
beach; one lurked on the
eastern side of Normanby
Wharf as late as the 1950s.
Behind the steam crane's jib
the steep path and handrails
can be seen winding up to the
lighthouse.*
– North Otago Museum 277

LEADER
— OAMARU —

amid the combined smells of a boiling-down works, a cattle factory and a sewage farm.'[12] Some would have come from ships' heads – few worried about that in 1923 – but most was Oamaru's own, piped south of the Cape only to be swept north in a filthy flow, some of which came in between the breakwater and the mole, where it lodged off the wharf. All subsequent dredge crews reported similar problems.

In 1938–9, as the Ramsay Extension crawled out into the Pacific, the harbour board improved both main wharves. It rebuilt the western approach to Holmes Wharf to make better use of the 50-metre landward 'dead' end, where the old track layout made it difficult to work rail wagons efficiently. The small boat landing stage, previously angled out, was also made parallel with the wharf. In November 1938, the Marine Department approved widening the

*Helped by the council and the harbour board, the Friendly Bay
Improvement Society cleaned up the western side of the harbour
between the wars. For several decades the old shop sold sweets
and ice creams over summer. – North Otago Museum 2765*

Record-breaker. The 10,107-ton Opawa *and the 10,048-ton* Otaio, *which called in 1938 and 1939, were Oamaru's largest visitors. Who, watching these magnificent modern motorships enter port, would have believed that Oamaru was about to lose the UK trade?* – North Otago Museum

curved approach to Sumpter Wharf to make it easier to shunt and load wagons.[13] By now Sumpter Wharf was used only when Holmes was congested. In 1935, the Railways district traffic manager reported that in the last twelve months Sumpter had handled only 7.64 per cent of the port's 31,000 tonnes of cargo. Nevertheless, since the very large Home boats would now tie up Holmes Wharf completely for several days, a back-up wharf was still required.

Had the board waited a couple of years it might have saved the money it spent on Sumpter's. But who could have predicted that the outbreak of the war, so long anticipated, would cause the permanent loss of the port's Home trade? Certainly not the Oamaru Harbour Board, which had been very successful recently in getting direct inwards calls from Conference Line ships. The port had never seen such large ships, the Ramsay Extension was under way, albeit more slowly than hoped, the economy had recovered, Oamaru had just been designated a wool appraisal port, and there was no reason to believe that the United Kingdom trade was at risk. The early months of the war brought few changes. Ships came and went the same as always, and some in the district even wondered whether this new war, like the South African War forty years earlier, might produce a bonus for the harbour.

Chapter Five

'A NAVIGATIONAL HAZARD'
1941–1974

Oamaru Harbour had not been defended in World War I – the threat from a handful of German raiders simply did not justify the cost. World War II was a different matter, though, and with the Imperial Japanese Navy rampaging through the Pacific in 1941–2, the government decided to make Oamaru a 'minor defended port'. In 1942, the Public Works Department started building an emplacement on Cape Wanbrow for a former U.S. Coastguard 5-inch (127-mm) 51-calibre gun. Construction proceeded slowly, complicated by the proximity of the old lighthouse, which had to be relocated. Finally, the battery (141 Heavy Battery RNZA) was complete and three proofing shots were fired in July 1943. The complex comprised the gun emplacement, observation post, magazine, mess and storeroom and it was manned by territorial gunners, supplemented by home guardsmen. But by now the Allies had the Japanese on the run, so the new battery was stepped down to care and maintenance four months later. The army removed the ammunition in September 1944 and sent the gun to Burnham Camp in January 1945, leaving the concrete structures as reminders of the brief war scare.[1]

Economics, not explosives, pummelled the port during the war. Many of Oamaru's regular traders painted over their bright peacetime livery, sprouted defensive weapons, and deserted their normal runs. For a year the Home boats kept calling – Shaw Savill & Albion's big *Coptic* and *Zealandic* in February and April 1940 respectively – so no one suspected that when the 8067-ton *Somerset* sailed on 7 November 1940 Oamaru had seen its last Home boat. With shipping in short supply, the government decided to rationalise port calls, delighting the Overseas Shipowners' Allotment Committee (OSAC), long resentful of the parochialism that spawned so many ports.

What tasted like champagne to OSAC was vinegar on the lips of the Oamaru Harbour Board. Remembering its World War I experience, it strongly opposed this downgrading, rightly suspecting that this 'temporary' measure would become permanent. For the next decade and a half, it would

World War 1 cost Oamaru its Home boat calls. This night photograph shows either the Tekoa *or (more likely because she called more frequently) the* Turakina *working at night. They typified the vessels built for the New Zealand Shipping Co and the Federal line in the early 1920s – big, no-frills floating freezers.*
– North Otago Museum

After the war Captain Jock Laird's Oamaru friends erected a memorial to the popular captain of the Turakina, *sunk by a German raider in the Tasman Sea in 1940. The memorial was moved to the Lookout in the 1980s.*
– Gavin McLean

Children paddle unconcerned in Surf Bay while the Ramsay Extension lies abandoned in the background.
– North Otago Museum 6758

lobby to have the calls reinstated, but with complete lack of success. Leadenhall Street, London, the shipping barons' home, did not want to hear. In 1946 Oamaru lost its status as a wool allocation centre, gained as recently as the eve of the war. As a sweetener, OSAC subsidised farmers to rail meat, wool and skins to Timaru or to Port Chalmers, pleasing the shippers but not the harbour board. And it was no use appealing to Wellington. In 1949, an interdepartmental committee investigating the secondary ports wrote that 'overseas ship owners … have raised objections to returning to Oamaru … and I think it would be unwise for your Board to anticipate the return of overseas vessels in the near future.'[2]

In 1943 the Public Works department finished this gun emplacement for an American 5-inch gun transferred through the Royal Navy. By then the threat of invasion had receded, so the battery was stood down after a few months. The Oamaru Coastal Defence Restoration Trust now looks after the site and plans further restoration and interpretation.
– Gavin McLean

After World War II a glimmer of hope appeared with the frozen meat run to Japan, which then used smaller ships. Oamaru shipped barley there aboard the 4362-ton *Yuho Maru* in December 1952, and in May 1958 exported tallow aboard the small Dutch ship *Van Cloon* to South-East Asia, but that was all. The Japan trade proved as elusive as the British one. A few years earlier, the influential Meat Board had reported that 'shipping companies are adamant that the port represents a navigational hazard to their vessels now serving the New Zealand trade.'[3]

Navigational hazards were on everyone's mind as the Ramsay Extension crumbled. Built on the cheap to a foreshortened design, it had made slow, uneven progress during the war. In 1941 workers made their best effort, reaching 95 metres. By next year it was 111 metres long, but as wave damage intensified further out, progress slowed and then halted. In 1943, a quarry accident killed two workers. The next year the board sealed off the extension, 43 metres short of the 1934 first stage, and 159 shy of Furkert's original length. Although the harbourmaster initially reported benefits from the extension, it was a white elephant. The trade it was designed to promote had gone, the harbour renewals fund was running dry, and the board now lacked the resources and the willpower to finish this embarrassment.

But could it simply abandon the extension? Some feared not. In the 1950s rumours flew through town that its debris – 'a mound of random stone rubble, faced on the seaward side with the largest stone in the Board's quarry, but with a core or hearting composed of material little better than quarry rubbish' – might spread into the entrance channel, halting shipping.[4] Others feared it was already damaging the breakwater by concentrating the full force of the waves into the pocket formed where it joined the older structure. Eventually the board determined that rock was not entering the channel, and it decided to let

In 1957 the quarry became a construction site for tetrapods. They have been made off and on ever since. The 14-tonne monsters were the brainchild of France's Laboratoire Dauphinois d'Hydraulique. Their distinctive shape dissipates wave action – water flows around rather than against them – and their legs interlock, making it harder for them to be washed away. – Gavin McLean collection; ship line drawing by Steve Lampard.

the extension disintegrate. In 1957, after a visit by French firm Neyrpic, it started armouring the seaward side of the breakwater and the extension with tetrapods. Fifty years later, Oamaru is still manufacturing them.

Board unity crumbled along with the extension as members formed factions around the harbourmaster and the secretary. At times it read like a bad farce. In February 1943 A.C. McLelland criticised chairman G T. Gillies for permitting the secretary to buy a bicycle for board business. Wartime rationing probably blew this out of proportion, but it was really a symptom of tensions between the secretary and the harbourmaster. McLelland had backed the harbourmaster and got stuck into the chairman's 'curly-headed boy' who (after twice being refused rationed tyres, a critic noted) 'is now flying about the streets on a Blue Streak'. Cries of 'nonsense!' and 'dictatorial' flew around the boardroom while Gillies told McLelland that he 'would take the latter out in the backyard if he were a younger man.'[5] Next month, McLelland attacked Gillies over the extension, claiming that the board had 'failed lamentably .[6]

It was a bad time to be squabbling, for there was even a fear that the trans-Tasman trade might be lost. No dredging had been carried out since the Otakou's charter in 1940 and reduced port depths, together with a shortage of shipping, made the Union Company reluctant to send ships to Oamaru. By 1947, however, the entrance had been increased to 7 metres, and the next year the Empire Dirk loaded the first wheat for Australia since 1939.

Nevertheless, the port statistics made bad reading. In 1947, ship calls (fifty-seven) were barely a third of 1937's tally. Fortunately, things were not as bad as port critics

'Forty-Seven Little Men Come to Oamaru.' Newspaper reports were less politically correct in December 1952 when the Oamaru Mail announced the port's only large postwar overseas visitor. The Yuho Maru, an old former British freighter, lies at Holmes Wharf in December 1952 while Oamaru and Timaru yachts battle it out in the foreground. – Graeme Ferris

The 1947–48 maiden four, later the senior four, ORC stalwarts until the mid 1950s. Left to right: John Gallagher, Rusty Robertson, Mick Logan and Brian Collett.
– Murray McLean collection

LAUNCHPAD FOR OLYMPIC GOLD

Oamaru Harbour's recreational users transformed themselves after the war. The oldest body, the Oamaru Boating Club, had, as in World War I, gone into wartime recess, closing the clubhouse from 1942 until the 1945–6 season.

In 1948, a year after the formation of the North Otago Yacht and Power Boat Club, the Boating Club changed its name to the Oamaru Rowing Club (ORC) to better reflect its activities. The ORC's old double wooden-gabled premises, with their uneven rock- and sand-covered floors, always seemed to fill with shingle after storms. Crews regularly cleaned them out, but the big floods caused by 1951's spring tides finally forced the club to commit itself to seeking drier grounds. But where? And with what? Fundraising took much longer than anyone expected, but thanks to the club's share of the profits from the Oamaru Christmas Carnival Association's Friendly Bay carnivals, ORC coach, local builder Russell 'Rusty' Robertson (1927–89) and Andy Paterson and volunteer workers completed modern concrete block premises in 1966 across the road on Marine Parade, safe from flooding. The old shed was demolished in two stages to allow the widening of the mole for the Holmes Wharf upgrade.

The ORC came into its own in the late 1950s, when it amassed a prize and trophy haul better than many much larger clubs. In 1961 and 1962 Win Stephens, Keith Hesselwood, Bill Smedley

claimed. Ship calls and cargo figures are very different things. Ports earn money from tonnage and berthage fees and from pilotage, call-driven, but their real bread and butter comes from handling cargo. So, although the tonnage of shipping arrivals fell from about 140–150,000 tons in the late 1930s to 50–60,000 tons in the late 1940s, cargo handled actually increased slightly, averaging in the high 30,000 tonnes in the late 1940s. the ships may have been fewer in number, and smaller, but they now moved more cargo on average. That is why Treasury had ignored the board's request for compensation for wartime centralisation. Treasury grouped ports into three categories: 'good' (five ports), 'position satisfactory meantime' (fourteen ports including Oamaru) and 'doubtful' (Wairoa, Wanganui and Bay of Islands). Its analysis of the OHB's accounts for 1936, 1939 and 1942 showed that harbour revenue (£4988, £4748 and £3294 respectively) had fallen less drastically than general expenditure (£6755, £11709 and £4411 respectively); in addition the board earned substantial income from rents and other sources, so '1942, with an excess of income over expenditure of £4293 is better than either 1936 or 1939, in each of which years an adverse balance is shown.'[7]

In 1947, the government set up the Waterfront Industry Commission (WIC) to improve waterfront efficiency and on 30 June Oamaru became the last port to get a waterfront central pay office. By 1951, WIC's sole Oamaru employee looked after the fifty-four workers on Oamaru's register, placing it above Picton (forty) and Onehunga (thirty-seven) on the secondary ports schedule. Of those fifty-four men, however, only forty were considered effective. At peak times and over the holiday, fourteen to fifteen non-union workers had to be brought in to make up the numbers. The board would have liked seventy men to work the trans-Tasman ships faster, but had no hope of getting them: breaks of two or three days between ship calls meant that Oamaru's wharfies earned less than their counterparts elsewhere – an average of £375 (worth $20,000 in 2007).

Port congestion and industrial unrest plagued the country's postwar years. Oamaru had none of the former

Facing page: Joan and Murray McLean (foreground left) take in the Friendly Bay Carnival in 1959. Note the much-travelled watchman's hut (see pages 28 and 31) – North Otago Museum

The four takes to the harbour in the early postwar era. Murray McLean in the bow seat. – Murray McLean collection

Perfect gentlemen. Competitors congratulate each other at Friendly Bay after a race. A big crowd lines the Esplanade, behind which can be seen the Carnival Association's sound shell.
Max Smyth collection, North Otago Museum

The Oamaru Rowing Club building.

and George Patterson won the New Zealand fours, and then gold at the Perth Empire and Commonwealth Games in the coxed fours with Douglas Pulman. Oamaru put out the red carpet for the golden boys. Robertson and his rowers marched up the Opera House stairs under a tunnel of oars before a crowd of 500 and Mayor Bill Laney exulted that on a per capita basis Oamaru had more representatives in the games team than any other town or city: 'so it can be safely said that we now have the greatest number of gold medals.'[8]

The 1960s and the 1970s were a golden era for the ORC, with its members representing New Zealand at most Olympic and Commonwealth games and with Rusty Robertson coaching the national team until after the 1976 Montreal Olympics.

and little of the latter, but port users felt the ripple effects of trouble elsewhere. Even so, the board was less interested in industrial strife than it was in regaining its export trade, using its submission to the commission of inquiry into the waterfront in January 1951, for example, to argue that sending overseas ships to Oamaru would relieve pressure on the main ports.

Interest in the royal commission was overtaken by the great waterfront lockout (or strike, depending on your politics), the last of New Zealand's great maritime disputes. 'The dispute took place in a climate of Cold War suspicion. The opposing sides denounced each other as Nazis, "commies", traitors and terrorists', NZHistory. net observes. 'It polarised politics and split the union movement, leaving a bitter legacy that lingers to this day. The combatants couldn't even agree on what to call the dispute – the employers and government described it as a strike, but to the waterside workers it was a lockout.'[9] One thing they could agree on was that it was serious. National Party Prime Minister Sid Holland used inflammatory language, alleging that the country was 'at war'.

The dispute was triggered when employers refused watersiders' demands for the 15 per cent cost of living increase the Arbitration Court had given other workers. On 9 February the union rejected 9 per cent. Four days later, it banned overtime; on 15 February, employers retaliated by imposing a two-day penalty. Events escalated: on 18 February, the ports came to a halt; two days later the government suspended the WIC; on 21 February, it declared a state of emergency and gave the wharfies until 26 February to return to work. When they stayed out, it sent troops to the Auckland and Wellington wharves (27 February), deregistered the Waterfront Workers' Union (28 February) and suspended its funds (2 March).

Oamaru Harbour was empty until 16 February, when the coaster *Waipahi* arrived to load for Nelson and New Plymouth. The day before, the Oamaru branch of the

For over a decade the coaster Tanea *was one of Oamaru's largest regular callers. This photograph shows her leaving port on 19 September 1962. Because she and the Union Company's* Kanna *filled Holmes Wharf, the* Turihaua *used Sumpter Wharf – the only time it handled cargo after the war. A year later, under the name* Holmbank, *the* Turihaua *sank off Banks Peninsula. Note the small sheds at the end of Holmes Wharf; harbour sheds came and went.– North Otago Museum*

union decided that no work would be done until the 19th or unless head office lifted the ban. Already most of its members were caught up in the dispute – twenty-three men, sent to work at Timaru, had been discharged and fined a two-day penalty for refusing overtime, and the remainder had been penalised a week's guaranteed wage for failing to go to Timaru.[10]

Now began a period of wait-and-see. 'We are waiting on the government to make the move', branch secretary

'Give us the ships, we'll load them!' the Union Company's Oamaru agent wrote on the back of this photo sent to head office. In May and June 1951 the Kauri spent a fortnight alongside Holmes Wharf loading a backlog of potatoes, oats, lime, flour and general cargo for Auckland. She left on 6 June 1951, loaded to the gunwales with 4219 tons of cargo, some of it lashed to the hatches. – Gavin McLean Collection

J.D. Hunter said on 25 February. It moved soon enough. On 2 March the branch's bank books and ledgers were seized. As the lockout intensified, Oamaru wharfies repeatedly reported for work, only to be sent home for upholding the overtime ban.

The wider community also suffered. On 9 March the *Otago Daily Times* reported layoffs at the Regina confectionery plant because sugar was running out. Throughout the town, sugar, coal and other basics were running low, while the warehouses were bursting with stranded goods.[11]

The *Waipahi* lay alongside Holmes Wharf for three weeks while the military concentrated on more crucial ports. Finally, on 9 April a naval crew flew from Auckland to sail the ship (the seamen were also striking) and soldiers from Burnham arrived to start loading cargo. The Union Company exalted to see her moving again, but the *Waipahi*'s departure was actually bad news for Oamaru. Since the government was putting its thin resources into ports that had ships to move, Oamaru, now empty, would be bypassed by the navy-manned skeleton coastal service until a new watersiders' union could guarantee to work any ships sent there. By mid-May local politicians were complaining about Oamaru cargo going elsewhere. The government sympathised but repeated its insistence on a new union at Oamaru. On 18 April an Essential Supplies Committee met, but merely prioritised freight to be railed to Timaru.

Oamaru was deeply divided. On 2 May, when the government called for volunteers for a 'Civil Emergency Organisation', 177 people signed up; two days later the number was 327. The press, controlled by the government, but anti-union anyway, alleged that many old unionists were itching to join a new one and get back to work. But when the Oamaru wharfies met on 12 May, they defied these predictions. Claiming an 85 per cent representation from the old union, the branch pledged 'its fullest support to the National Union.'[12]

What happened next is difficult to unravel given censorship, press bias and inadequate records. On Monday 14 May, only two days after the members of the deregistered branch rejected forming a new one, one did appear. It was registered the next day in Wellington and a Labour Department official claimed that 'the presence of a good proportion of the members of the old union had considerably strengthened the new organisation.' Now the coaster *Breeze* could be sent to the port, berthing at 1030 on the 17th to load for Wanganui. Three gangs worked her, a mix of new unionists and casual labourers, the latter recruited through newspaper appeals. But how many were members of the old union as government officials claimed? Probably not many. Early that afternoon 20 to 25 deregistered unionists – at least half the old union's strength – subjected the new workers to 'abusive language and intimidation' before being dispersed by police.

Oil tanks shine in the sun. In the 1950s all the major companies built fuel depots at the waterfront, taking advantage of the Tanea's *visits. – Max Smythe collection, North Otago Museum 306*

When the *Breeze* sailed on the 19th, agent H. Hay congratulated the watersiders for their efforts. Two days later, the *Kauri* arrived to load for Auckland. The Port of Oamaru was working again, although things were not back to normal. Little is known about Oamaru's locked-out workers, but they probably experienced financial and emotional hardship of the kind reported by families at Port Chalmers and elsewhere. The confrontation at the wharf showed that feelings ran deep. The WIC had changed the locks on the watersiders' waiting room on Holmes Wharf and employers seem to have victimised men from the old union. James Revelley's book shows that Oamaru was one of the ports with the highest percentage of deregistered unionists excluded by employers – the others were Auckland (where employers made a special effort), Dunedin (but not Port Chalmers in the same harbour) and Picton, Napier and Gisborne.[13] The new unionists inherited the new waiting room constructed by WIC in the 1951–52 financial year.

Not long after, the port gained a new trade, oil. Shell had had a small tanker on the coast since 1927, the *Paua*, but she seldom visited Oamaru. In 1950 it brought in the 3060-ton, 100-metre-long ship *Tanea*. Initially she did not call at Oamaru, which had no bulk oil tanks. Nevertheless, on her maiden voyage in November 1950, she swung in close to the breakwater to 'make her bow to that port' and radioed Shell's Oamaru Shell branch, 'Greetings from the *Tanea*.' 'With ensign, ship's numbers and house flag flying we circled off the entrance to the harbour, giving several long blasts on the whistle before proceeding', Captain D.R. Patterson recalled.[14] The ship began calling from 9 December 1953 to service Shell's new bulk installation on the reclamation. For the next eleven years she was one of Oamaru's biggest regulars, contributing significantly to port profits by pumping 5–6000 tonnes of oil across the wharf. The opening of the Marsden Point refinery in 1964 spelled the end for oil deliveries to Oamaru, since the new 12–13,000-ton coastal tankers were too big to enter port.

In 1965, in the initial upgrade of the wharf, the pipeline was removed from Holmes Wharf, to the relief of the fire brigade, and the regret of the harbour board. It could not afford to lose staple cargoes.

But the late 1950s had brought a series of blows to the port. In 1957 the overseas shipping lines, which had been subsidising the railing of North Otago meat to Timaru since centralising exports, announced a staged withdrawal of that payment. The axing of this subsidy had the ring of finality: Oamaru could forget any aspirations of regaining export port status for anything beyond Australia. In 1957, too, a major flour producer announced plans to move its production to the North Island, taking away 25 per cent of the port's throughput.

Two years later, tragedy struck when a regular caller sank just north of the port, with the loss of all aboard. On the evening of 24 November 1959, Captain Henry Williams of the *Tanea* and Oamaru harbourmaster Captain John Hancox visited the home of Shell Oil's local manager. On their way there, 'an exceptionally violent south westerly squall' passed over Oamaru, nearly blowing them

to their feet. 'I expressed to Captain Hancox at the time how wise we were to have cancelled the *Tanea*'s sailing as we could well have been caught on the knuckle of the wharf', Williams recalled.[15] By the time they reached the house, news was breaking that the ship that had sailed from Oamaru that afternoon, the coaster *Holmglen*, had radioed: 'Heeling hard to port ... accommodation awash. Crew attempting to launch boat,' before going silent.

Soon a small fleet was searching the South Canterbury coastline in appalling gale-force conditions. The Oamaru fishing boat *Venture* joined several freighters, navy launches and fishing boats from Akaroa and Timaru. The wreck was located by echo-sounder, lying in fifty-five metres of water just north of the Waitaki River mouth.

The *Holmglen* had a crew of 15, and her loss left owner Captain John Holm, stunned: '*Holmglen* was the strongest built and the best equipped ship in New Zealand.' She had sailed from Oamaru at 1540 hours with a mixed cargo from Dunedin and Oamaru. The seas were moderate and although she was heavily laden and carrying deck cargo, she was above her marks. 'I was impressed with her general appearance, everything being apparently well stowed and lashed in a seamanlike manner', Captain Williams later testified, 'she was stowed in a stable position.'[16]

That deck cargo attracted considerable attention. The *Holmglen* was licensed to carry 50 tons (50.8 tonnes), and had about 28.5 tonnes on deck, lashed to the No. 1 hatch, tucked in behind the forecastle. In an initial report, the Oamaru superintendent of mercantile marine thought that the order in which the oats and flour were stowed on deck was unusual. He also reported that 'the engine room door on the *Holmglen* was unlatched when the vessel left Oamaru', but at the inquiry witnesses agreed that the cargo was safely stowed.[17] Allan McKay, president of the wharfies, recalled hearing the chief officer tell the foreman to pump out a ballast tank to compensate for the deck cargo. 'I heard the remark that this tank would give 30 tons and I got the order to continue loading.'[18] Eric

Tutty, the foreman, confirmed following the first officer's instructions and did not see any water in the hold.

Former officers and seamen testified that the *Holmglen* performed badly in heavy seas. In May 1958 while crossing Cook Strait, a deck cargo of coke had broken loose and blocked the scuppers and wash ports, forcing the deck crew to jettison the sacks on the port side to clear the wash ports and get rid of the water. Had this happened and the *Holmglen* broached? Rowland Masterman said that 'she was under-powered and would almost stop in anything of a sea. She would ship water quite heavily over the bulwarks, forward of the mast housing.'[19] J.D. Garrick, former crewman, called the *Holmglen* 'a rock and roll ship'.[20] Alex Grieve, her former master, however, considered her seaworthy and Holm's marine superintendent thought 'she wasn't good [at steering], but she wasn't notoriously bad. She was an average little coaster.'[21]

An underwater camera survey failed to find an obvious answer. The *Holmglen* sat upright on the seabed. A staysail (sometimes used to steady the ship under certain sea conditions) was rigged. Both hatches were sound and secure. The starboard weather door leading from C hatch deck along past the master's cabin was wide open but not clipped. All wheelhouse doors and windows were closed, as were all port holes. The port sea boat was secured. The starboard one was missing (it had been recovered floating on the surface) but its davits had not been turned out, indicating that it had not been launched by the crew. The only visible damage was trivial, minor crushing of guard rail stanchions, guard rails and the railing around the ladder leading from the accommodation deck to the boat deck.

The court failed to find the cause for the catastrophe, which was debated by mariners for years to come. Most agreed that the *Holmglen*, always considered 'cranky', had

The Holmglen*'s mast (top) filmed by a navy underwater camera. – Gavin McLean collection*

BANANA BOATS

On 4 July 1974 Oamaru finally regained a brief stake in t[
frozen meat export trade. The ship, the *Ata*, had been delay[
a day by engine trouble at Timaru and, when photograph[
alongside Holmes Wharf loading the historic shipment, bare
poked above the wharf.

The *Ata* was tiny, 67 tons gross and a mere 25.6 metres lon
little bigger than the Timaru stern trawler *Moray Rose*, a freque
port visitor in the 1970s. The *Ata* was a converted trawler, n
surprising considering that her owners, the Warner Pacific Li
of Tonga, had been a fishing firm until branching into shippi[
recently, entering the New Zealand trade about a year earli[
bringing bananas and taking back meat, vegetables and buildi[

lost way, been overwhelmed by a sudden wind gust, and had sunk when the cargo shifted. Captain E.F. Rainbow, a former master, believed that the *Holmglen*, running before a heavy southerly sea, pooped a sea which flooded the galley and saloon, then poured down the accommodation ladder into the officers' quarters. Before she could recover, she pooped a second sea and sank stern-first, explaining why neither lifeboat had been untied, since it would have been impossible to stand upright and perform this activity.[22]

The harbour board blamed the loss of the *Holmglen* and severe fire damage to the *Holmburn* for a downturn in its trade during the 1959–60 financial year. Holm's short-term problems led to it withdrawing from the Oamaru to Wanganui and New Plymouth early in 1961 and things were not helped by the Union Company's having to lay up the *Karu* because of a shortage of engineers.[23] But new ships were entering service: the *Storm* (1960), *Pukeko* (1961) and the *Holmglen*'s bigger replacement, the *Holmdale* (1961), as well as several ships for the Northern Steam Ship Co's new East Coast trade, which had included Oamaru from the time of the first visits by the *Hotunui* and the *Tainui* in May and June 1955 respectively.[24] Nevertheless, board members were growing more worried. 'A Harbour Board is nothing in itself but is entirely dependent on ships and shipping for its prosperity and the residents must be made to realise the seriousness of the position and act according', the 1957 annual report

Afternoon sunlight illuminates the sister ships Kanna *and* Katui *alongside Holmes Wharf in the early 1960s. These 925-ton freighters had been designed by the Royal Navy as supply ships for service in South-East Asia but were bought on the stocks by the Union Company, which ran between Auckland and South Island ports between 1946 and 1967. It is estimated that they made about 400 calls to Oamaru.*
– Gavin McLean collection

The Ata, *photographed from the breakwater.* – *Gavin McLean*

products. She had called to load a trial 25-tonne shipment of meat from Waitaki's Pukeuri freezing works.

A fortnight later Warner's bigger, new ship *Frysna* also put in an appearance. The *Frysna* was smaller than the coasters serving the port but at 298 tons gross at least looked like a proper ship. Aboard her was the line's managing-director, Peter Warner, keen to meet the town's exporters to see if Oamaru could be added to the line's schedule, which was currently Lyttelton and Timaru. Warner called Oamaru 'a nice little port where everyone co-operates', but was not so positive about the watersider union's Wellington head office, which required the *Frysna* to work a full gang of twenty-four wharfies. They took just an hour to load the thirty-five tonnes of frozen meat, yet had to be paid for a minimum of five hours' work.

Warner Pacific ships paid several more calls between July 1973 and February 1974, when Oamaru was dropped from the schedule. It was not surprising: the *Ata* had a crew of ten but could carry only 28 tonnes of cargo!

From the 1960s the Union Company transferred the Oamaru trade to its subsidiary companies, which operated modern Dutch and British-built coasters. Most were engines-aft designs, like Richardson & Co's Parera *(823 tons, 1957), which features in both pictures and the Canterbury Steam Shipping Co's* Storm *(931 tons, 1960). The ship on the left, however, the* Holmwood *(797 tons, 1953) was, like the* Holmdale, *a three-island (forecastle, midships bridge and poop) design, by now considered old-fashioned. – North Otago Museum*

Seagulls line the ropes between the Kanna *and a larger Union Company freighter.*
– Max Smythe collection, North Otago Museum 305

had warned. 'If it is the wish of the community that the Port should die of sleeping sickness they have only to carry on in the present spirit of apathy.'[25]

While coastal arrivals slumped from 102 ships in 1959 to eighty-five in 1960 and eighty-one in 1961, they bounced back up to 106 in 1962. By then the board had another problem on its hands – the shallowing entrance. The *Karu* touched lightly while entering on 26 October 1963, the *Holmlea* on 26 March 1964, and the *Holmburn* on 6 May 1964. No harm was done, but the incidents were embarrassing, so the board chartered Wanganui's dredge for four months in 1963, another month in 1963 and in 1966 used Timaru's big new dredge *W.H. Orbell* to clean out a massive 113,000 tonnes of silt and shingle over a three-month period.[26]

More worrying than the arrivals figures were the cargo statistics, down from 51,404 tonnes in 1958 to 43,078 in 1960, a level it more or less maintained for several years before dropping again as the new Cook Strait rail ferries made their presence felt. Far away in Europe and in North America, naval architects and shipping companies had revolutionised cargo ships for the first time in nearly a century. Containers, roll-on, roll-off, pallets, all-weather meat loaders, these were some of the new concepts to cut costs and to speed ship turnaround. The conventional ship, despite its mechanical steel hatch covers, electric deck cranes and high-speed engines, had reached the end of its technological development. It was struggling to cope with the surge in international trade. All over the globe, fast modern streamlined freighters were wasting time and money alongside congested wharves.

New solutions were needed, ships like the Railway Department's Cook Strait roll-on, roll-off passenger/cargo ferry *Aramoana*. In 1962 this ship (and the *Aranui* of 1966) finally meshed together the North and South Island main trunk lines with a steel, seagoing bridge. Until then, rail was no threat to shipping, since freight crossing Cook Strait had to be unloaded from wagons into ships

on one side and unloaded and re-stowed in another wagon on the other. Rail ferries made the crossing seamless and undermined conventional ships in non-bulk trades, since the train/ferry combo was faster and could deliver rail wagons straight to manufacturers' rail sidings, especially good news for the growing inland towns of Palmerston North and Hamilton. Convenience, cost and speed – rail now had it all over the old-fashioned coaster, especially when Railways and private sector freight-forwarders offered train/truck package deals. The last blow came when the Labour Government froze railway charges at a time of soaring oil prices and high inflation.

The Union Company's Konini *swings off the berth on her way to northern ports. She was built in 1957 by Henry Robb of Leith and served until made redundant by roll-on, roll-off ships in 1971. – Oamaru Mail collection, North Otago Museum*

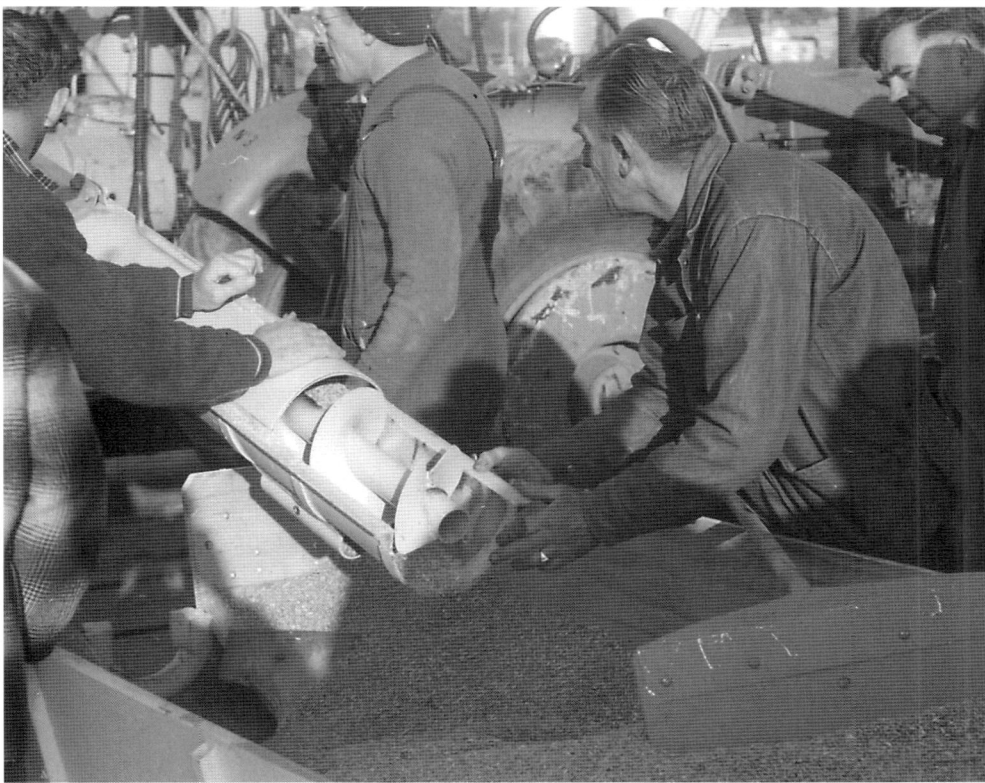

These 1967 photographs show watersiders loading the first bulk grain cargo to leave the port – aboard the coaster Calm. – *Oamaru Mail Collection, North Otago Museum*

The shipping lines had few remedies. Although Oamaru never handled containers (apart from the Holm Shipping Company's mini-boxes) or roll-on, roll-off ships, in the early 1960s the Northern Company experimented with unloading cargo direct on to trucks rather than into rail wagons. When the *Awanui* discharged alcohol into New Zealand Express Co trucks late in 1963, Wellington's *Evening Post* reported the event as 'a progressive step for Oamaru.' From now on, beer shipments for the Oamaru Licensing Trust would be shipped on steel pallets and loaded on to trucks.[27]

In 1949 the Rivercrest*'s master refused to discharge Australian wheat at Oamaru, sparking fears for the Australian, or 'intercolonial' trade, as the board quaintly called it. Nevertheless, Australian cargo crossed Holmes Wharf until 1973, mostly grain and iron. The Union Company's* Waimea *(above, 3657 tons, 1953) traded between Melbourne and South Island ports. She was a traditional 'slow green', with a forest of tall union purchase cargo derricks. The* Karetu *(opposite, 3222 tons, 1964), sported modern deck cranes – the only such ship to visit Oamaru. – Oamaru Mail collection, North Otago Museum*

Tug and barges were another new technology. In May 1971 the tug *Unit Shipper*, which ran a roll-on, roll-off barge service between Timaru and Onehunga against the maritime unions' opposition and intense rail competition, visited Oamaru to examine the port while her barge loaded at Timaru. She berthed at Holmes Wharf, raising a few brief hopes, but never returned. Within a year the company went out of business.

Holmes Wharf was not suited to articulated trucks, so in 1965, against ratepayer opposition, the board borrowed $180,000 to upgrade it. The north mole was widened at the landward end and also to allow trucks to turn and leave the wharf by going around the buildings without interfering with vehicles or wagons on the wharf. Berthing arrangements were also changed to accommodate three instead of two 1000-ton coasters. Bulk shipment of grain in converted coasters made this work more essential than ever, since much of the grain came by truck. The redevelopment, which included repiling and strengthening, was finished in 1971, delayed by the need to service shipping. Cargo throughput held up surprisingly well until 1970, when the figures tumbled. Between 1964 and 1969, port throughput had averaged between 30,000 and 37,000 tonnes, depending on grain harvests and exports. In 1970, however, tonnage slid to 20,094 tonnes, fell again but stabilised in the 12,500–11,600 range in 1971 and 1972, and then fell to 7471 tonnes in 1973 and a mere 584 tonnes in 1974.

By then the port was on its last legs. The commissioning of the third and fourth rail ferries in 1969 and 1974 dealt knock-out blows to the coastal fleet, and by the middle of 1973 Oamaru was down to a monthly visit by the *Storm* on the Napier/Gisborne route. In a sign of the times, the Union Company transferred ship agency work to its Dunedin office.

The grain season brought calls by the *Awanui*, but they disappeared when the harbour entrance shallowed after heavy storms in July. An estimated 10–12,000 tonnes of kelp lay on the Oamaru foreshore, rotting unpleasantly in the wintry sun, but the real damage was less visible, out in the channel. There the wild weather had pushed the board's old nemesis, the shingle bank off the breakwater head, westwards, reducing the depth from 4.9 metres at low tide to just under 4.3 metres. Although high tide brought that up to six metres, that was insufficient for the Northern Company, which cancelled the *Awanui*'s mid-August call. Until channel depths improved, its ships would stay away.[28] Since Northern was looking at larger ships, it stated its preference for 7.5 metres of depth and for wheat silos on the wharf. Despite this, on 21 September the Union Company's much bigger (3790 tons) *Koraki* brought in pig iron for the foundry. This was Oamaru's last trans-Tasman caller – or 'intercolonial', as the Oamaru Harbour Board's berthage register still put it. She drew 4.3 metres and unloaded 864 tonnes of cargo in thirteen hours.

The board could afford to dredge, but decided to wait until coastal shipping's future looked more certain. It was just as well, because government talk about coastal tug and barge services – the American-owned Dillingham Corporation was discussing a joint venture with several harbour boards – came to nothing. Oamaru's trade was dying. Imports had virtually ceased and flour was now virtually the only cargo going out. In the financial year ended 30 September, cargo fell from the low 11,600 tonnes to 10,161 tonnes; port revenue ($10,277) and income from rents and interest ($18,520) fell far short of outgoings ($41,288).

The *Holmdale* took over from the *Storm*, running a coastal voyage in between her monthly Chatham Island supply run. On 14 May 1974, she pulled away from Holmes Wharf for the last time. No one took much notice, because further calls were planned. The *Holmdale* was due to call in June but more storms reduced entrance depths, so her Oamaru cargo was railed to Timaru for loading.[29]

November 1970 was unusually busy. Between September and November the SEDCO 135-F oil rig drilled just off the port, supported by the tug Willem Barendsz (seen leaving port) and the supply ships Min Tide and Canadian Tide (pictured). They made sixty-one entrances to this crowded port, which was then being deepened by the dredge Ngamotu, seen at the entrance. The freighter Pukeko is working the outer berth. The photograph (left) of the Min Tide is a rarity – the only time Normanby Wharf handled cargo after the war.
– Otago Daily Times and Oamaru Mail collection, North Otago Museum

The ships that had served the port barely outlived it. In November and December 1974, the Northern Company, battered by the 1974 collapse of the South Island grain trade, withdrew its last ships. The Union Company, which had absorbed the Canterbury Steam, Holm Shipping and Richardsons coasters into its general cargo fleet, had been withdrawing them since 1971. In quick succession, formerly regular visitors were laid up and sold. In 1975 alone, the Storm, Holmburn, Parera and Pukeko were 'sold East'. Only a government subsidy kept the Holmdale running to the Chathams.

The departure of the Holmdale confirmed the 1866 prediction of crotchety old William Thomson that Otago would become a one-port province. Thomson foresaw a web of rail lines feeding Otago Harbour, making every other Otago port redundant. It took a century longer than he expected, thanks to trucks as much as trains, but the unthinkable in 1866 was finally reality. Otago Harbour was the region's only commercial port.

But what about Oamaru? No Otago port had closed in about ninety years, so the big question was, could the town maintain the breakwater and wharves now that its commercial revenue had dried up?

Final call. The Holmdale *loads at Oamaru for the last time in May 1974. – Oamaru Mail*

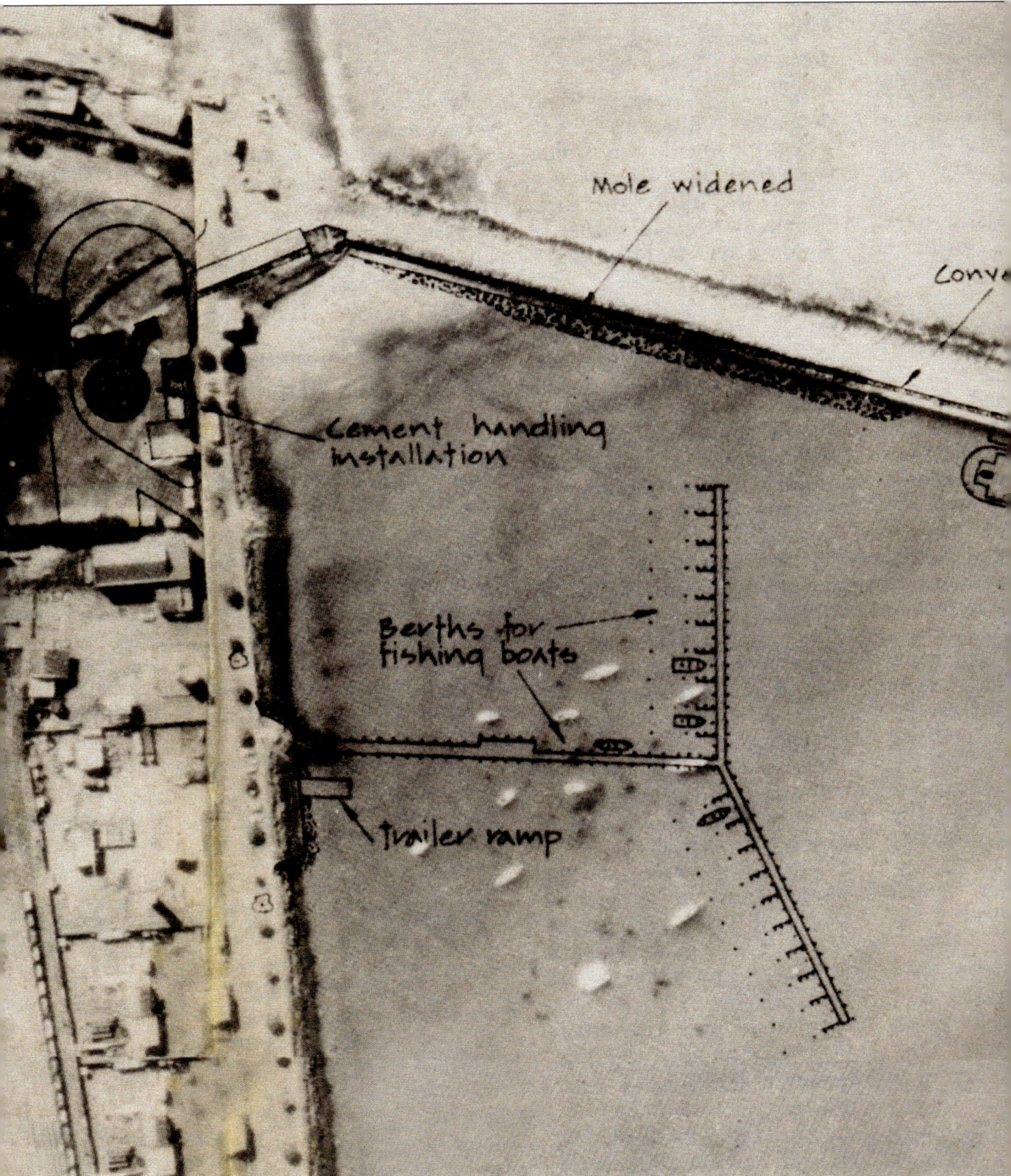

Mole widened

Conv[...]

Cement handling installation

Berths for fishing boats

trailer ramp

Chapter Six

'FINGERS CROSSED ENGINEERING'
1974–2008

It was as if, in blowing the dust from an ancient Ouija board, someone had accidentally summoned up a Victorian indignation meeting. On a dismally wet June evening in 1983, 750 people crowded into the Oamaru Opera House for some good old-fashioned parochial braying and blood-letting. Reg Denny, wearing his mayoral chains of office like armour, had summoned up the spirits which were howling like banshees. Flanking him on stage was every 'suit' he could muster, including Dunedin's mayor, repaying North Otago for backing the recent Port Chalmers container port bid.

Why were they baying for blood? Like so much in those days, it was against a decision made in Wellington, in this case the New Zealand Ports Authority. Few but shipping insiders knew much about the Authority, created in the 1960s to control capital expenditure by harbour boards. Now, however, Oamaruvians were up in arms. By dismissing New Zealand Cement Holding's $7,549,000 application to re-open Oamaru Harbour to serve a planned cement works, the Authority had jeopardised 140 new North Otago jobs, since the company insisted: no port, no plant. Inside the Opera House, local MP Jonathan Elworthy, a Cabinet minister holding a very marginal seat, tiptoed nervously along a fraying political tightrope. Away from Wellington, he called the Authority 'a relatively unimportant group', and expediently hammered its 'narrow point of view.'[1] It was music to the ears of locals, who overwhelmingly backed the call for a ministerial review. 'When the chips are down and bureaucrats threatens [sic] to stifle development in our region, you have shown we will not be beaten without a fight', the *Oamaru Mail* crowed, its enthusiasm getting the better of its grammar.

Its readers were angry. Very. North Otago sat atop centuries' worth of prime limestone. For decades people had seen this as the port's salvation, since it was too bulky to rail or truck. In November 1965, at a secret meeting, a Cement Holdings director had advised the Oamaru Harbour Board

Plan for a new cement wharf for Oamaru, published by the Oamaru Mail *in 1982.*
— *Oamaru Mail, Gavin McLean Collection*

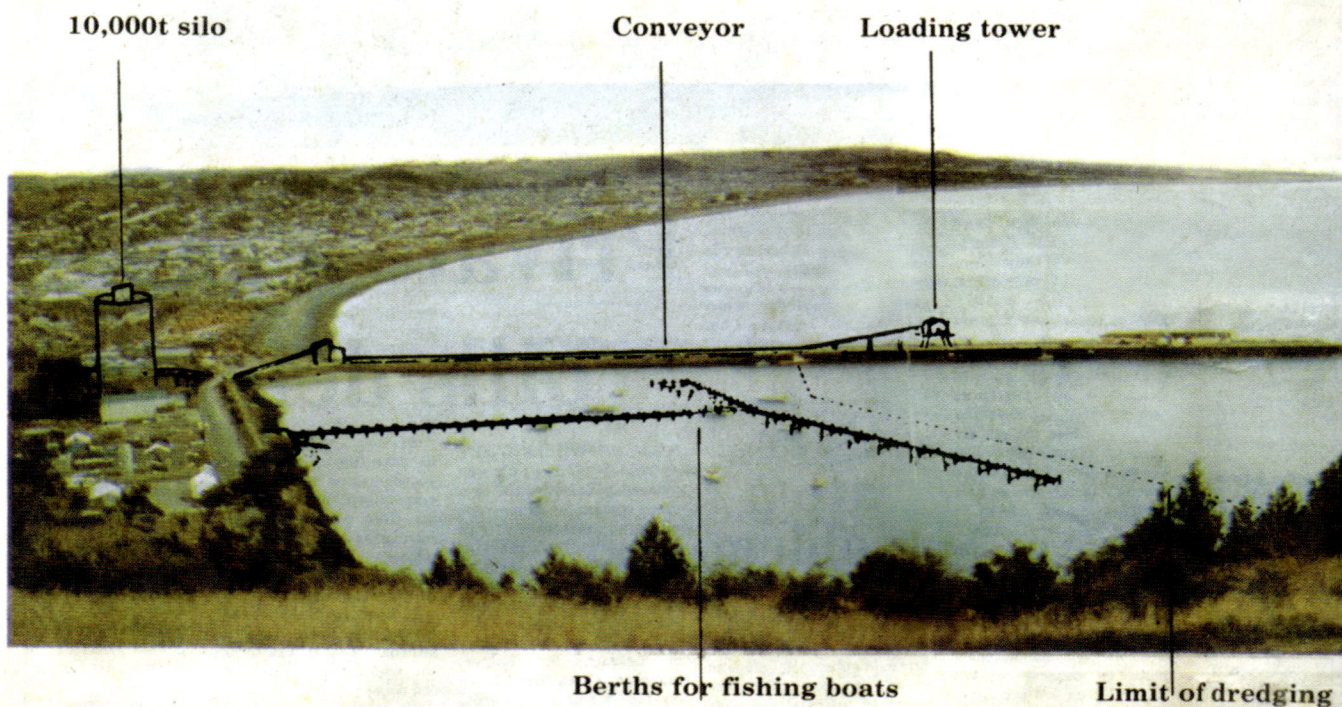

10,000t silo   Conveyor   Loading tower

Berths for fishing boats   Limit of dredging

of its plans to replace its old Burnside (Dunedin) works. Trial borings showed that the Oamaru foreshore would support cement silos, so the board waited patiently as the company bought land and sought funding and planning approvals.[2] Twelve years later, Cement Holdings finally announced plans for a $75 million plant at Weston, just inland from Oamaru. It would be Milburn's first new technology dry process facility. But a recession obliged Cement Holdings to defer construction. Elworthy's government added the plant to its controversial 'Think Big' development programme and a confident harbour board purred that 'the port itself looks to a new era – the 1980s and beyond – with the promise of ships to call.'[3]

First, though, it would have to circumvent the Ports Authority, which had viewed with increasing disfavour the 'wasteful' competition between Golden Bay Cement and Cement Holdings, especially when they built silos side-by-side at ports. The Authority also wanted to use Weston's cement to give a breathing space to Timaru, which had recently lost much of its export trade to the new Lyttelton and Port Chalmers container terminals. It also objected to North Otago ratepayers contributing to developing a single-user port facility.

Politicians reacted to this prescription of economic rationalism like vampires to garlic. The Ports Authority Act 1968 included an appeal process, so on a grey, wintry July day, grey, muffled politicians and officials glumly walked along the breakwater, inspecting the facilities and listening to locals. In public, Minister of Transport George Gair said little, aware of his judicial position as the appeal authority, but he would have felt the political pulse of this very marginal seat. At the appeal meeting in August, therefore, they cooked up a face-saving compromise. Timaru and the Railways (which had offered discounted rates between Weston and Timaru) accepted Oamaru's re-opening for coastal shipments if Timaru got the small export bagged trade.[4] This verbal footwork enabled everyone except the Ports Authority to feign smiles for the cameras.

At first sight, the development plans prepared by E.R. Garden & Partners Ltd were impressive. Cement Holdings had looked at more radical proposals, even simulating wave tank modelling tests for breakwater extensions, but it settled on a relatively conservative upgrade to let fully-laden bulk carriers sail two hours either side of high water. The business side of the plan, a council/company joint project, was to add a new loading berth (eighty-five metres long and an extra four metres wide) served by a loading tower on Holmes Wharf. The tower was connected to a 38-metre-high, 10,000-tonne capacity cement silo behind Friendly Bay, fed by an enclosed conveyor belt on a slightly raised rocky berm alongside the edge of the mole. A second berth could be used for ships awaiting loading, or for

**Raised breakwater —
New armouring on seaward side**

pter wharf to be demolished

Scissors, glue and marker pens. In 1982, before the days of computer generated image packages, the Oamaru Mail *sketched E.R. Garden & Partners' plans for a cement port: demolishing Sumpter Wharf to make it easier to turn ships inside the harbour and installing a conveyor to transport cement from a 38-metre-high silo behind Friendly Bay to a ship loading tower on Holmes Wharf.*
– Oamaru Mail, *Gavin McLean Collection*

unloading gypsum. The berths would serve 100-metre-long ships and Sumpter Wharf would be demolished to enlarge the swinging basin. Initial dredging would create a shipping channel seven metres deep at low water, though that could be bettered; 320,000 cubic metres would be removed by a trailer suction hopper dredge and 10,000 cubic metres by a wharf-operated grab.

Other changes were relatively minor. Fishing boats displaced from Holmes and Sumpter wharves would get a new Y-shaped floating jetty off Marine Parade near the site of the old dredging jetty. Boats would moor bow-in and would work cargo against the long jetty arm. There would also be a launching ramp. On the southern side of the harbour, the seawall would be repaired and the slipway upgraded. The seaward section of the breakwater would be heightened by two metres and armouring reinstated all along the structure and the remains of the Ramsay Extension.

The applicants got their consents, but could not make the figures work. The wheels had fallen off Prime Minister Robert Muldoon's heavily regulated economy. Labour, elected in 1984, ripped off those controls. In the uncertainty that followed, 'it was not easy to arrange finance for the project. The New Zealand dollar was devalued 20% in 1984 and inflation rose to 17% in 1985.' The domestic price of cement was still regulated and

barely covered production costs and the state's cement-hungry hydro construction schemes were running down. When the Swiss gnomes got nervous, 'the Oamaru plan was quietly shelved.'[5]

The slow, silent death of the cement works was bad news for the harbour board, which, just weeks after farewelling its last ship, celebrated its centenary with a dinner and the unveiling of a commemorative plaque donated by former chairman G.T. Gillies. In the harbour, where HMNZS *Inverell* flew the flag for the navy, the North Otago Yacht and Power Boat Club opened a new

Milestone or tombstone? By the time G.T. Gillies unveiled the OHB centennial plaque, the port's trade was dead. – Gavin McLean

After 1974 the trawler South Wind *was the largest regular port user. Here the boat powers into port in light summer winds.*
– *Gavin McLean*

Sunk by a shed. The tip of the Edie's *mast pokes up off the launch steps after waves washed the old Union Company gear store off Holmes Wharf. The harbour board's lines launch swings serenely at her moorings.* – *North Otago Museum*

boat ramp by the slipway. A month later the Waitaki County Council county clerk took over as harbour board secretary-manager, with the board's unhappy secretary (A.A. Bird) transferring to the county, in return for the board paying the county an annual administration fee.

The joint statement issued by the board and county promised that the board would continue to meet as usual. But what was usual? Soon even the old men meeting in the board's crumbling Italianate office sensed that there was something Monty Pythonish about gathering there every month to preside solemnly over an empty harbour. But what could they do? Since they insisted on retaining local control, they could not hand over the port to the Timaru or Otago harbour boards. They wanted joint administration by Oamaru borough and the Waitaki and Waimate county councils, but rating by multiple authorities was not permissible, so after talking to the Ports Authority and the Local Government Commission they gave the harbour to the borough, which created an oversight committee that included representatives of the two counties. On 2 March 1978 the order dissolving the Oamaru Harbour Board was gazetted, effective from 31 March. That night its members consigned its 103 years and eight months to history at a farewell dinner.

The new harbour committee, chaired by former board chairman J.H. Mitchell, met on 28 April 1978. It was a case of new administration, same problems: 'perhaps ironically, the committee set as its number one works priority the maintenance and repair of the breakwater.'[6] Although the board had left adequate reserves, with the real revenue-earners, the ships, gone, the committee now had to maintain the port on mooring fees, shed rentals and levies on crates of fish.

To make matters worse, some 'assets' were liabilities. Ferocious storms in August 1973 had reduced the entrance to a depth of 4.25 metres at low water on the line of leads. The board could still afford to dredge, but held

back because of the uncertain state of coastal shipping. As a result, the shoaling off the breakwater tip worsened. This was bad news to Captain A. Grieve, Timaru's harbourmaster, who had also been looking after Oamaru since 1972, when harbourmaster Captain Jim MacLean resigned. Grieve's connection with Oamaru went back further than that, for he had briefly piloted ships there a decade earlier, when Captain Jim Hancox resigned after the board compulsorily retired foreman John Campbell. By 1975, the shingle build-up was threatening even the fishing boats. That October, Grieve advised the Marine Division of the Ministry of Transport (MOT) to warn mariners to keep well west of the main leads. The shingle bank, which

Ironically, even as the harbour board struggled to attract shipping, it had one 'customer' too many. Early in 1974 the thirty-seven year old powered lighter Kaiwaka *(169 tons) arrived for repairs after a stint as a venison recovery ship. By May her owner had twice been told to remove her. As the harbour master considered that Sumpter Wharf 'is a bit ancient, and is becoming too weak to bear the weight of the* Kaiwaka', *she moved to Holmes Wharf, where she was equally unwelcome. Letters flew back and forth, but the* Kaiwaka *nevertheless spent a couple of years at Oamaru.*
– Gavin McLean

dried in places alongside the breakwater at low water, was spreading into part of the shipping channel demarcated by the leads.[7] The soundings taken by Bill Owen, the leading hand, showed an inexorable deterioration: 3.4 metres at low water on the line of leads in July 1975, 2.7 metres in April 1976, 2.1 metres in April 1977.[8] Although the swinging basin and the Holmes Wharf berths were still deep, the entrance was worse than in any time in the port's history.

While local skippers adapted to the situation, Grieve worried that boats now had to keep west of the leads and sail along the eastern side of the North Mole to cut in sharply towards the harbour entrance – 'a precarious manoeuvre in rough weather or on very dark night.'[9] What about visitors unfamiliar with the entrance? In 2007, he recalled 'being rowed out to the harbour entrance in line with the leads then stepping out of the boat and taking soundings, in my gum boots, with a 4' stick!!'[10]

By 1987 Grieve's patience with the harbour committee was exhausted: one of the worst moments had been the special meeting called to authorise key-holders for the new gate at the entrance to the wharf.[11] Earlier, frustrated by its refusal to dredge, he got the MOT to add a warning to the charts against entering port without first contacting him. 'Since that time several fishing boats have reported striking the bottom on entering or leaving port and one fishing boat has been sunk', he complained to harbour committee secretary J. Rudhall. 'It would appear that the Harbour Committee are ignoring pleas to remove the shingle by dredging and so give safe access under these circumstances ... I therefore intend advising the Ministry that I shall no longer act as Harbour Master of the Port of Oamaru and that in my opinion the port should be closed to shipping.'[12]

Ministry advisers trawled through the legislation and decided that they could not close the port to fishermen. But they did the next best thing, amending

the Notice to Mariners to read: 'Oamaru Harbour is no longer open to shipping, and is dangerous for small craft because of extensive shoaling in the entrance.'[13] But the harbour committee scarcely blinked. It was struggling to find $300,000 for urgent repairs to the breakwater and could not afford to dredge. In March 1986 engineering consultant Ian Robertson aptly described port administration as 'fingers crossed engineering ... living within the tight budget and hoping no major cost projects came up.' A committee member muttered that 'the whole thing depends on the cement works' – an increasingly vain hope.[14] Borough overseer Lawrence Hardy became honorary harbourmaster (a position he relinquished in February 1997) but with neither the budget, nor the political will, to create one, maintenance was purely reactive.[15] On 5 February 1988, for example, the now-misleading leading marks were removed from Cape Wanbrow.

Oamaru Roulette. In 1973 a 4000-ton ship safely entered port. Thirteen years later, small launches had to judge their entrances carefully as the shingle fan spreading out from the breakwater choked most of the entrance channel. The rollers, breaking across those shallows, force the Enterprise *in against the rocks of the mole (right), requiring a swift course change to clear the Holmes Wharf dolphin (opposite).* – Graeme Ferris

Fishermen made the most of a bad deal. On 6 June 1987, reporting the flare-up, Wellington's *Evening Post* said that there were 'six big trawlers' from Timaru and nine local boats alongside Holmes Wharf, and that the Sanford processing plant on Normanby Wharf was busy. 'There's plenty of occasions when you couldn't get out of the harbour because the entrance would get filled with shingle', Syd Tangney explained in 1996.[16] On 17 December 1991, after 5-to 6-metre swells generated by Cyclone Val prevented the *Clan Cameron* and *Kaipara* from entering port, North Otago Search & Rescue Controller John McLellan warned that a serious accident looked inevitable. Not too ruffled by his enforced night at sea, Ron Wilson, the *Clan Cameron*'s skipper, agreed that 'if there had been a wind blowing last night we might really have been at panic stations.'[17]

The shoaling was just another blow to the fishery. Like most inshore operators, North Otago fishers noticed the hammering that stocks took as big foreign trawlers plundered the seas. By the late 1970s, the signs of resource depletion were becoming apparent and in 1986 the government created a quota management system to manage commercially harvested species. It was a leading-edge scheme and has been credited with arresting the slide of several stocks, but its implementation cost time and money. Boat owners grizzled about all the extra paperwork. 'Things have got a lot tougher,' Tangney said in 1996. 'We got quota based on our catch history in the preceding years but the quota system took away the freedom. Every fish that gets caught has to be written in the book. It turned it into an office job trying to keep track of everything. The fish stocks have been pretty lean the last couple of years.'[18]

Opposite: The fishing boat Clan Cameron *entering port easily at high water in the early 1980s. In December 1991, however, it was a different story and she had to spend the night at sea until conditions were safe to enter.*
Gavin McLean

The need to address the shoaling at the entrance finally arrested the drift that had characterised harbour administration for so many years. By the mid 1990s, the entrance was less than a metre deep at low tide. The bigger boats now had only a one-to-two-hour window either side of high tide to enter or leave port. Worse, they had to cut perilously close to the rocky outer edge of Holmes Wharf, making the operation especially dangerous in swells.

Some harbour watchers believed that the harbour committee had coasted idly, waiting for Cement Holdings to rescue the port. If so, that attitude began to change in the mid-1990s, when it became apparent that the cement plant plans were anything but concrete. Oamaru would have to take responsibility for its harbour. In 1996,

therefore, Leo Breen, property manager for the Waitaki District Council (created from the 1989 merger of the Oamaru Borough Council and the Waitaki County Council), prepared a 5- to 10-year strategy for the harbour. Proposals to double the harbour rate brought predictable howls from the hinterland, but in October the works committee supported a $1.12 million development plan; the main items were $720,000 for breakwater/ Ramsay Extension repairs, $160,000 for Holmes Wharf and $100,000 for dredging the entrance to four metres at low water.[19] Exploratory quantities of sand had been removed from the entrance and from Surf Bay, and in early 1995 a dozen redundant shipping containers had been filled with concrete and placed along damaged parts

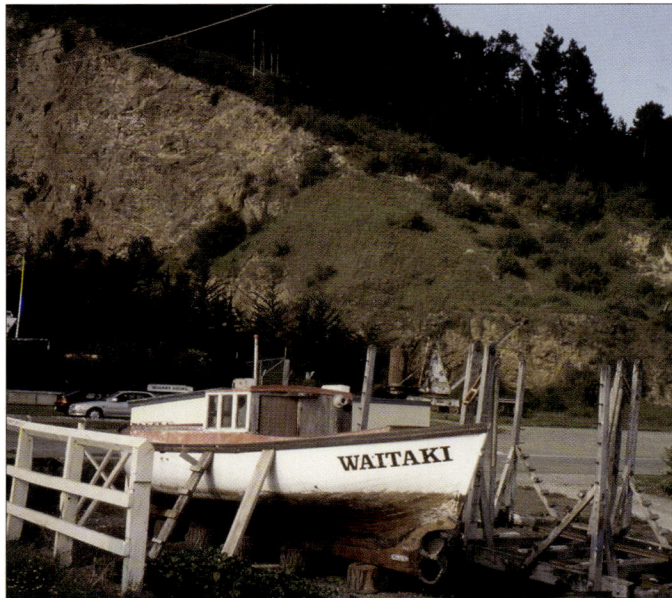

Washed-up. The Waitaki *on the slip in 2004 after sinking. Although she had not fished commercially for years, this classic doubled-ender had been part of the harbour for eight decades.*
– Gavin McLean

of the breakwater. Later that year the full council agreed to keep the harbour open and maintain the breakwater to safeguard the commercial area from erosion.

This decision was a boon to the town's growing fleet of small craft, increasingly recreational rather than commercial. Fishing boats still use the port, in decreasing numbers, Timaru boats to unload catch, and the handful of local boats and a charter launch. Commercial operators now vie with each other to protect favourite groper patches from recreational fishers in fizz-boats. Small in number they may be, but the town's fishers remain closest to the Victorians who created the harbour. Like the skippers of cutters and ketches scarcely larger than their own boats, they know the coast intimately. They also know to treat it with respect. When southerly winter storms sweep in mountainous seas, not even the breakwater and mole are always enough. Several boats have sunk lately, most recently the veteran launch *Waitaki*, which sank at her mooring one night in August 2004. She was salvaged next day, beached at Friendly Bay, pumped out and slipped.

Local fishers went through a particularly rough patch in 2003 and in 2004. On 11 May 2003, five men launched their six-metre aluminium boat *Time Out* from the slipway and sped out to Hepburns, a popular fishing ground near Kakanui Point. They left in fine weather, but it deteriorated in the middle of the morning. The *Time*

Out was well-equipped, but she was too small for three-metre south-west swells. Unfortunately, a fishing line wrapped itself around her propeller and she capsized while it was being cleared. Two Timaruvians died in the chilly water. The incident was widely reported and provoked intense debate about emergency services' response times. The coroner found that the men should have put on lifejackets when the weather deteriorated and headed home sooner.[20]

Disaster struck once more a few months later. At 6 a.m. on 21 January 2004, forty-four-year old Ian Paul Tangney took the *Moana* out to the Hepburns. In contrast to the aluminium speedster *Time Out*, the 9.8-metre *Moana* was a tough, traditional-style carvel-planked launch from Miller & Tunnage's Port Chalmers shipyard. She was thirty-four years old and small, but she was seaworthy and well equipped, for the Tangneys took no chances.

So why did it all go wrong? We will never know for sure. The weather was fine and the slight sea swell should not have troubled the *Moana*. Paul Tangney was last seen, still fishing, at 3.15 p.m. Around mid-afternoon he phoned the Sanford plant on Normanby Wharf to say he had had a good day and was heading home. Those were his last words. Father Syd, who was expecting him back at 6 p.m., became concerned when he did not receive the usual homecoming call. He contacted search and rescue co-ordinator John McLellan from Moeraki, who raised the alarm.

Cape Wanbrow residents Pat and Joan Winders went for a walk that evening. Around 6.30 p.m., Pat saw a flash at sea, which he believed to be the sun reflecting off a boat's windscreen. About an hour later, back at their house, he was paged about the rescue. Joan scanned the sea and saw a boat, but no sign of an occupant. It was 'struggling' and was 'all over the place'. When she returned from the police station at 8.05 p.m., she saw that it was now travelling in clockwise circles. Shortly after seeing either steam or smoke coming from the boat, she lost sight of it.

Divers located the *Moana* at a depth of twenty-four metres, eleven kilometres off the Kakanui coast. Her engine was in gear, and the VHF and the radio were turned on. The emergency locator beacon had not been activated. Coroner George Berry had few details to offer. 'The best one speculates is there's been a mishap of some kind … and Paul has been lost over the side … It just seems to go with the territory. From time to time, even to the best, most careful fishermen, accidents will happen.'[21] The Maritime Safety Authority report recommended wearing lifejackets on fishing boats – the new inflatable, less restrictive types now available. Syd Tangney was not convinced: 'I fished for about 50 years and the first time I wore a life jacket was on the Shotover Jet.'[22]

That was one less port user, but at least by the end of the century boats could use the port in relative safety. Over April and May 1997 the entrance had been dredged for the first time since 1971. Port Otago Ltd's small tug *Kopu* and crane barge *Vulcan* removed 5512 cubic metres of shingle and sand at the rate of three to four loads a day, taking the entrance channel below four metres at low water. Port Otago was busy next time the council tendered, so Daniel Smith Industries carried out the work over the summer of 2003–4. In 2000, the navy's 9.7-metre inshore SMB (survey motor boat) *Adventure* spent over three months at Oamaru, surveying the harbour and the approaches to the port.

Toll of the sea. In May 2004 the wrecked fishing boat Moana *was refloated, towed into port and beached off Friendly Bay, where friends placed bunches of flowers and a bottle of beer on her deck as tributes. The wheelhouse and part of the deck were missing, but tenderer Glen Perham had her battered hull hauled up on to the slipway for eventual restoration. – Graeme Ferris*

Oamaru's chart was the last in the country to change from fathoms to metres.

Restoration of channel depths enabled other naval vessels to resume their visits, the inshore patrol craft (IPC) HMNZS *Moa* calling for the first time since 1985. In following years, the *Moa* and other IPCs paid occasional calls. On 9 June 2006 twenty people gathered on Holmes Wharf to greet two IPCs, HMNZS *Wakakura*, patrolling the EEZ, and HMNZS *Moa*, Auckland-bound for decommissioning. The boats offered the greatest concentration of 'shipping' at the port for years. Even though they drew only 2.4 metres, the *Otago Daily Times* noted that they had to wait for high tide to enter. The council's harbour activity management plan calls for regular dredging to maintain four metres low-water draft, just ahead of the introduction of new, larger inshore patrol vessels (IPVs) to replace the IPCs, which the *Mail* said will be 'too big to fit in Oamaru Harbour.'[23]

The counterpoint to the other recurring strain in the harbour's history was, of course, the breakwater blues. The same storms that pushed shingle into the channel battered the breakwater. Although the commercial trade it was designed to protect had vanished, and experts considered that it had exceeded its life expectancy, it still performed a vital job protecting the harbour and the foreshore around central Oamaru. In the twentieth century the town and the Railways Department had struggled to prevent coastal erosion north of the harbour and in 2006 the partial collapse of rock protective walls and accelerating erosion threatened the old 1886 freezing works building. 'If erosion continues at this rate it won't be long before there will be water in the main street', Historic Places Trust

Botched, bastardised … Macandrew Wharf in 2002 after ill-conceived 'repairs' that damaged the heritage values of this historic place. – Gavin McLean

(HPT) branch chairman Ken Mitchell warned.[24]

Centuries ago, Queen Mary is said to have declared that after her death the word 'Calais' (then an English outpost in France) would be found engraved on her heart. Post-mortems of Oamaru politicians might find the word 'breakwater' on theirs. Storms in the 1970s and the 1980s had caused sleepless nights, but those of July–August 2001 were unusually destructive, requiring expensive repairs to a very visible gap. Unfortunately, the work, which damaged the registered historic place, was botched. The WDC chief executive's 2003–4 report explained that 'an external review of the work by Opus International Consultants Ltd was critical of the value and effectiveness of a substantial portion of the repair works.' The chief executive resigned.

The Opus report sparked a comprehensive review of options, from a $1.4 million 'managed deterioration' to a $17.1 million full structural upgrade. In 2004, the council's preferred option was $4.3 million for monitoring and repairing the structure as far as the Ramsay Extension

and constructing a berm breakwater on the harbour side north of that, leaving the historic structure to erode. 'The design philosophy for a berm breakwater allowed for lighter rock than required for a traditional breakwater to be placed in bulk and be shaped by wave action to a stable profile,' the *Otago Daily Times* reported. 'The berm breakwater would be formed on higher ground, thus saving materials. Periodically, part of the berm would be washed away. To minimise this, denser rock than that available locally would be sought.'[25]

In 2005, consultants using divers revealed three areas of damage requiring urgent repairs. The most pressing, just north of the Ramsay Extension, was a crack in the breakwater. There they recommended driving sheet piling in front of the structure, forcing in concrete grouting behind to fill gaps and bind the blocks; in the longer term they recommended building a rock wall beside it and using tetrapods to reduce wave impact. Tetrapods should also protect the Ramsay Extension's remains, and closer to the landward end a breach would be repaired by inserting a container and pouring reinforced concrete. Rock armouring around the penguin colony would also be strengthened.[26]

In late 2005, therefore, the council had the tetrapod moulds, unused for years, cleaned and painted. The following year, it contracted Fulton Hogan to build 150 tetrapods, the first of 500 or more needed. In June 2007 Rooney Earthmoving Ltd won the $659,000 contract to place 190 tetrapods around the Ramsay Extension, concrete a damaged section of the breakwater, and put 10-tonne armour rocks at the outer end. Work began on creating a rock 'road' on the breakwater's inner-edge to provide access for mobile cranes.

By then any lingering hopes of a cement port had vanished. In the new century, the booming economy and the limitations of its ageing Westport works prompted Cement Holdings (now known as Holcim) to take a fresh look at Weston. But Oamaru Harbour was no longer part of its plan, because the amount of dredging required to reopen it, 'challenges with road/rail connections and the close location of heritage buildings and wildlife.[27] Since much of the plant's output may be exported in big bulk carriers, North Otago cement is likely to be railed to Timaru for distribution. That probably sounds the death knell on use of the port by commercial shipping in the near future, although mounting concerns about climate change and carbon emissions cannot rule out future reuse. The government's November 2007 *Sea Change* strategy paper called for doubling coastal shipping's share of domestic freight haulage to 30 per cent by 2030. There is just the faintest chance that Captain Thomson's prediction of a single port for Otago might yet be reversed.

'THERE'S NOUGHT TO FEAR FOR THE PORT OF OAMARU?'

'Oamaru, fair Oamaru; The port of Oamaru;
We tell you here there's nought to fear
For the port of Oamaru'

Thirty years ago the cement company would not have factored heritage into its decision-making. Now it did. The harbour was enjoying greater public recognition after a long period of neglect. After ships stopped calling in 1974, Oamaru virtually turned its back on the waterfront. Jobs vanished from the wharves and the oil tanks came down. A 75-tonne tank towed to Timaru in March 1979 by Captain Grieve in the tug *Aorangi* was the last 'cargo' to leave the port. Only the wool stores by Sumpter Wharf, the fishing boats, and the fish plant on Normanby Wharf kept anyone working on or by the sea.

The waterfront deteriorated. Paint flaked from buildings and the northerly swells picked away at the seawalls, at Marine Parade and at the old wooden fences. Sumpter Wharf's decking got shakier and its boat landing decayed. Eventually even the last of the fishing launches shifted across to Holmes Wharf or to moorings out in the harbour. Surf Bay and the Cross Wharf silted up. Even the Friendly Bay Christmas carnival decamped to Takaro Park in the centre of town, where it quietly expired. The old tearooms closed. After high seas and vandals had had their run at making eyesores of them and the nearby public toilets, council bulldozers completed the job. 'Today the area is largely deserted – gone are the café where icecreams were sold, the runabouts sheltered by ngaio trees, the rowing sheds, the band rotunda and the tennis courts', *Kingdom By the Sea: Janet Frame's Oamaru* observed in 1997.[1] It was derelict, dead.

A sea change took place in the early 1990s when locals, the Department of Conservation (DOC) and the Waitaki District Council joined forces to build a penguin viewing colony in the quarry. For years environmentalists, led by the tenacious Lorraine Adams, had campaigned to clean up the waterfront and to protect blue penguins from marauding dogs and from careless motorists. Yellow-eyed penguins (*Megadyptes antipodes*, or hoiho) nest around the Cape at Bushy Beach, but the blue penguin, *Eudyptula minor*, rules the roost here. It is the world's smallest penguin, a mere

Derelict deco. After the port closed, Oamaru turned its back on the waterfront, which crumbled under the onslaught of weather, neglect and vandalism. In 2006 these art deco-style lamp posts, built by the Improvement Society between the wars, awaited restoration. The concrete boat ramp to the right occupies the site of the old Dredging Jetty built to help the Progress's reclamation work

– Gavin McLean

NATURE'S INVADERS

Many creatures make use of this artificial, concrete-bound port, from the rabbits that sometimes bound around the wharves to Oamaru's new cash-cow, the little blue penguins.

The penguin colony has grown rapidly since 1992. That year Department of Conservation staff and volunteers planted shrubs, built soil mounds in the old harbour board quarry floor and installed nest boxes. Safe and secure in the penguin version of nappy valley, breeding pairs have increased from 33 to over 120. The Oamaru Blue Penguin Colony opened with makeshift viewing stands but grew as visitor numbers swelled. In 2001 it

You do not need to pay to see blue penguins or even wait for dark. They are all around the waterfront, the historic precinct, the lagoon and even on the landward side of Thames Street where they roost beneath the buildings provided so obligingly by businesses and householders. I photographed the one on the left from the Graves Walkway at 3.00 p.m. on a Sunday; the one below was sitting in

a discarded box behind the Woolstore at 9.00 the next morning as trucks sped by. A few days later the seal below was playing round the piles of Sumpter Wharf.
– Gavin McLean 2007

opened an attractive new visitor information centre (shown after extensions in 2006). A year later it completed a new viewing stand whose aesthetics, in contrast, would be more appropriate to a fast food outlet in a suburban mall than to an historic area. In 2006 it extended the information centre and opened a new boardwalk for daytime visitors. The year before, 42,000 people attended evening sessions and over 25,000 made daylight visits, keeping the cash registers singing.

kilogram in weight. It is also very common. Blues live all around the harbour, under rocks, wharves and buildings, where they can be a nuisance, even interrupting choir practice as far away as St Luke's. They are noisy and noisome (to use a good Victorian euphemism for smelly).

Blues hunt at sea by day and return to their nests at night. Oamaru's may have swum as much as twenty-five kilometres offshore and put in a seventy-five kilometre

workout during the day. They are a goldmine to moteliers, since the timing of their dusk promenades encourages tourists to overnight in town. Although bird numbers peak during the breeding season (September–January), they can be seen all year.

Like much of the post-industrial West, Oamaru grew more dependent on tourist dollars in the dying days of the twentieth century. That trend is likely to continue while

Graves Walkway edges round the loess cliffs past Boatman's Harbour on Cape Wanbrow. The walkway and beaches are an excellent place to see penguins and other marine life. They were dear to the heart of Oamaru solicitor and explorer William Grave (1874–1934) who sweated away for five years, often alone or with the help of a handful of friends, to form this walkway. The cliff was so steep in places that he had to lower himself by rope to work. The track was completed using relief labour during the Great Depression. – Gavin McLean 2003

oil prices remain affordable. In 2007 the development board estimated that the district's income from visitors would climb $50 million to $177 million by 2011. Some of that money is spent outside the town, but even there, 'green' (natural) heritage outperforms 'brown' (historic) heritage. Who would have predicted that twenty years ago in a town that is awash with Historic Places Trust Category I registrations?

Buildings, not birds, were tourism's first hope in the late 1980s as industry and farming slumped in the newly deregulated economy and the government slashed public sector jobs. Oamaru's population fell by over ten per cent. Not surprisingly, therefore, heritage tourism seemed a lifeline to a struggling town burdened with dozens of underutilised historic buildings. Oamaru's many boosters included novelist Maurice Shadbolt, who likened the old Harbour/Tyne Street precinct to a deserted film set. In 1988, therefore, the Oamaru Whitestone Civic Trust was formed to buy, restore and tenant the precinct,

which it did with considerable success. Victorian-garbed shopkeepers and tourists replaced storemen and coal yard labourers, and the exuberant Victorian parapets reappeared atop the old grain stores. Victoriana was hip, and Oamaru starred in movies, television commercials and magazine spreads.

Shadbolt's stage had come to life, but out in the wings little stirred. Although the precinct had served the port that created it, few people appreciated its relationship with the harbour, slumbering peacefully across the rusting

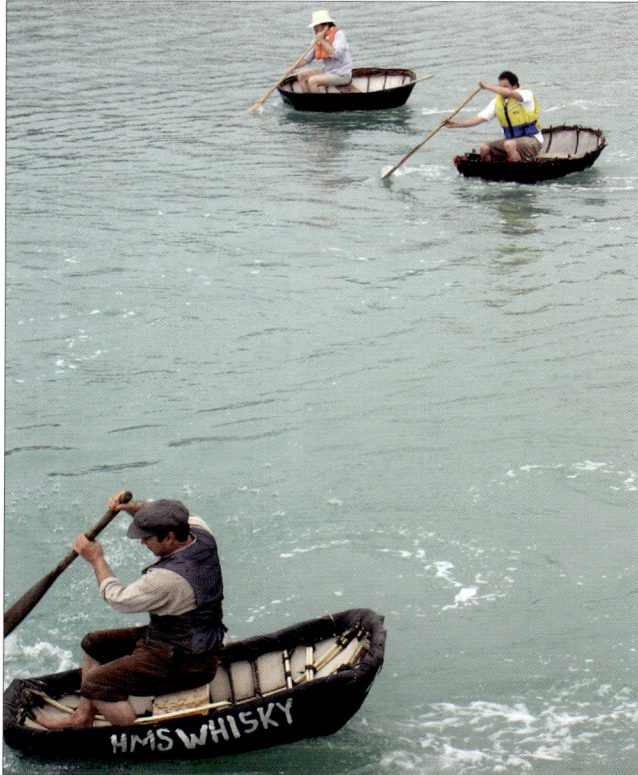

Christmas drinkers savour the last rays of the day in front of the restored Criterion Hotel (1877). – *Gavin McLean*

Coracles and miracles? In a town that celebrates its British heritage, it was perhaps inevitable that someone would revive interest in that most ancient of craft, the coracle. Dean Preston in HMS Whisky *participates in the December 2007 southern hemisphere championships.* – *Gavin McLean*

rail tracks, scrub and wild fennel. The breakwater's engineering significance had earned it a Category II, but in a town bristling with Greek columns and fancy Italianate parapets, that counted for little.

Things changed in the new century. Indeed, by 2004, when the HPT registered Oamaru Harbour as an historic area, many people were eyeing World Heritage status. Would Governor Grey's 'fair maiden' find her place alongside the pyramids, Angkor Wat, Stonehenge and the 800 other icons on one of the world's premier A-lists?

There were many bureaucratic hoops to jump through, starting with the Department of Conservation. For years DOC had run World Heritage like Dickens's Court of Chancery, and had given New Zealand's World Heritage List a DOC estate flavour: Fiordland National Park and Aoraki/Mt Cook & Westland/Tai Poutini National Parks, Tongariro National Park, and the country's sub-Antarctic islands scarcely reflected New Zealand history. Late that year, however, under fire from heritage groups, DOC extracted the departmental digit. Its consultation

document presented six illustrative sites – 'Oamaru port and CBD', the Papamoa pa complex, Napier's art deco precinct, the Waitangi Treaty Grounds, and two natural heritage sites, the Kermadec Islands and marine reserve, and Kahurangi National Park and Farewell Spit – as examples of the places that might be nominated.

DOC received 138 'substantive' and 149 'form' submissions. It promised that the 'final tentative list will be completed ready for submission to the World Heritage Committee by early 2006', but release dates came and went like the tides.[2] Finally, in late June 2007 DOC revealed its recommendations: Kahurangi National Park, Farewell Spit, Waikoropupu Springs and the Canaan Karst system; waters and seabed of the Fiords of Fiordland; Napier's Art Deco historic precinct; Kerikeri Basin; Waitangi Treaty Grounds; Kermadec Islands and Marine Reserve; Auckland Volcanic Field; and the North-East Islands (including Poor Knights Islands).[3]

Again, natural heritage had fared better than cultural heritage. Oamaru 'came close to being included in the recommended tentative list', but its international significance eluded DOC. Nor did the department comprehend 'the exact role and significance of the port in the development of the frozen meat trade and other exports' or savvy the significance of the land between Humber Street and the sea, containing amongst other things, the old freezing works. Locals vowed to try again. 'World heritage dream far from over' CHImp (the Culture and Heritage Implementation Group) vowed in 2007 as it studied best practice guidelines for managing World Heritage sites.[4]

Those guidelines might have come in handy down at the harbour, where ad hoc tinkering may have made heritage assessors question the local commitment to protecting heritage. The damage done to Macandrew Wharf by the bungled breakwater repairs of 2001 is still obvious. So, too, are the new buildings scattered across

the oldest part of the harbour like road kill: the penguin colony structures, and from 2006 the Harbour 2 Ocean restaurant (reopened as the less upmarket Portside Restaurant and Bar in early 2008) sprawled like a downed sumo wrestler across the eastern end of the historic Cross Wharf. It had been erected controversially after acquiring on a technicality a long-term lease over prime public waterfront space in a non-notified process. To add to the old wharf's indignities, the sea scouts were shunted aside into glorified aluminium garden sheds. Everywhere around the harbour unsightly, intrusive gates, fences and warning notices proliferated, and in 2007 people wanting to walk the restored Graves Walkway or see the pillow lava at Boatman's Harbour had to wait for the penguin colony to open since they were now obliged to traipse through its shop to get to the beach.

Nor was this all. In 2005 the council demolished Holmes Wharf's eastern tip during wharf 'repairs'. In 2007 leading Oamaruvians spent time reading their evidence in the Environment Court for and against a 2005 decision to sanction a non-complying activity, apartments in the wool stores. Developers had been sniffing around them for years. In 2004 they backed away, but when public purchase attempts failed, they applied to build a 15-apartment complex common to post-industrial waterfront makeovers. Despite objections that their 'Cormorants on Waterfront' was hatching a cuckoo in the heritage nest, a commissioner approved it, based in part on his own version of history in which 'accommodation,

while not at this density, was available for the harbour master, the night watchman and the lighthouse keeper in this particular port.'[5] The Civic Trust appealed to the Environment Court.

But not everything was negative. Despite the stoush between the council and the Civic Trust over the wool stores, the broader environment showed signs of the emergence of a more integrated approach to harbour protection and management. In February 2005 the council released a draft harbour development strategy. Its most important feature was to improve waterfront access by extending Wansbeck Street across the redundant railway land, effectively linking the southern end of the historic precinct to the port, enticing visitors to drive or walk (via the restored railway over-bridge) there. The Marine Parade lights and the harbour seawall would be restored, along with Sumpter Wharf. Areas for potential commercial development included the railway yards, the old grain silo area behind Friendly Bay, and 'limited small-scale development' along Waterfront Road around Sumpter and Normanby Wharf. It would also permit the contentious residential development 'in existing buildings within the precinct'.[6]

One of the more positive features was recognition for Sumpter Wharf, mouldering away behind 'keep out' signs. As its fiftieth anniversary project, the Historic Places Trust's North Otago branch paid marine engineer Nick Barber to inspect the wharf. He reported that he had 'never seen a wooden wharf that old in such reasonable

From ship to shop. The Harbour 2 Ocean restaurant (2006) squats heavily on Cross Wharf (1879) at the edge of a silting Surf Bay. Here, as elsewhere, the middle-class fetish for shopping, sipping and sleeping on global warming's front line sparks debates over development and land use. – Gavin McLean

condition.'[7] While the decking was decayed, most piles and cross braces were sound. His conservation plan envisaged reinstating the curved viaduct, re-decking the wharf and providing vehicle access to inner lay-up berths. SWAG (the Sumpter Wharf Action Group) planned to raise funds for the work, to be managed by a new trust – the council lacking confidence in the Whitestone Civic Trust's leadership.

Also in 2007 the council-led Harbourside Implementation Group agreed on a harbour development plan. This required a plan change, redesignating land around the harbour within Tyne and Test Streets, including Harbour Street, into a single new Harbourside Zone, replacing three existing zones.

As this book goes to press, therefore, the harbour may be entering a new era after three decades in limbo, completing the transition from the smokestack industrial economy to the servicing economy, from shipping to shopping. The heritage skirmishes taking place are symptoms of that process, as people adapt to new opportunities, launch new businesses and shape new vocabularies to describe their experiences and aspirations. The disagreements over public access to the waterfront, heritage preservation and wildlife protection reflect on a smaller scale debates happening throughout urban New Zealand and around the world.

Make no mistake, this is urban New Zealand. Oamaru's carefully preserved historic precinct, and its harbour, with its museum-piece steam crane and train, may appear quaint in a pre-cell phone, pre-internet kind of way. They make suitable backdrops to 'feel good' nostalgic television advertisements, but they were once places where the future was forged, where some people even predicted living to see docks to match London's famed system. Here, at the Pacific's edge, from a rough colonial beach-head, Oamaruvians saw their first mechanised transport (steamships in 1859), the world's second-largest steam travelling crane (1873), first railway (the breakwater line

in 1873) and first telephone (the harbour board's line to the breakwater in 1878). They expected to see more of the same.

That was the Victorian way. While aesthetes like William Morris pleaded to preserve the past, most Victorians pulled it down, built big, and contentedly sniffed the coal smoke. When the Rev. Alexander Todd admired North Otago in 1875, he gave thanks for the ploughed fields, homesteads, ships in the bay and the railway, all 'indications of civilisation', improvements on 'the dismal Maori period'. This was what historian James Belich calls the progress industry, with all the bells and (steam) whistles. Oamaru went along for the ride with a gusto exemplified by the harbour board's common seal: its top portion showed a ship snug behind the breakwater, steam crane busy at work; the lower panel featured the exports of the district, bags of wheat, bales of wool and blocks of stone. Suspended overhead was the Golden Fleece.

In the twenty-first century something more than sheep need to be fleeced to sustain a modern economy. Oamaru, once a Belich 'protein port', Cumberland's 'Kiwitown', has almost forgotten its lofty Victorian aspirations; who could imagine it rivalling the Port of London? Even the regional crowns went to Timaru and Otago, with their deeper ports and their bigger hinterlands. Nevertheless, Oamaru's story is exhilarating, epitomising the extraordinary vibrancy of coastal, colonial New Zealand: 'men and women, steam machines and (London) money pushing and pulling the whole amazing edifice onward and upward – and downward and sideways, but always running fast and frenetic like the headless chook in Katherine Mansfield's story.'[8] In Harbour Street the pace has slowed to a tourist's walk-and-gawp, but this town, which grew from nothing to the country's seventh-largest in a single generation, still preserves the physical traces of that mad mushroom boom better than most places. What better place to explore Kiwitown and its port?

Appendix 1

Oamaru Harbour Timeline

1854

January *Endeavour* made the first known call at Oamaru.

1858

Otago provincial government built a public store and derrick at the foot of the Cape.

1859

Subsidised steam shipping service commenced between Dunedin and Oamaru.

1861

1 August, Oamaru became a port of entry for Customs purposes.

1865

December, Foundation stone laid for the Oamaru jetty.

1868

4–5 February, jetty destroyed in a storm that also wrecked three ships.

1869

Oamaru Rocket Brigade formed.

1871

Oamaru Dock Trust formed.

1872

Construction of the breakwater commenced.

1874

Oamaru Harbour Board takes over from the Oamaru Dock Trust; Cape Wanbrow light commissioned 1 December.

1875

May, first section (46 metres) of Macandrew Wharf officially opened and named.

1876

Breakwater reached 192 metres (m). Macandrew Wharf extended to 100 m; inner berth offered 3.4 m depth at low water, outer berth 4.9 m. Otago Provincial Government abolished.

1878

Normanby Wharf completed; breakwater reached 286 m. Cape Wanbrow lighthouse changed from a fixed white light to a fixed red light.

1879

Cross Wharf completed and Normanby Wharf inner berth alterations finished. Thomas Forrester's survey of the seabed showed that dredging was practical.

1880

16 May, site for the North Mole fixed. Macfarlane and Watson awarded contract.

1881

21 January, barque *Ardentinny* sails for London, the first wool ship to load at Macandrew Wharf; Davidson & Conyers of Dunedin won a £12,000 contract to supply a steam dredge from Appleby Brothers (UK); Davidson & Conyers later became insolvent and the contract was transferred to Briscoe & Co of Dunedin. North Mole contract transferred to A.& J. Macfarlane and G. Watson of Dunedin.

1883

30 May, the dredge arrived at Oamaru, and was named *Progress* 31 May. 17 September, Philips & Jones of Timaru began building the new export wharf (Sumpter Wharf).

1884

August, Sumpter Wharf completed. September, North Mole finished(489.5 mtres long along the top, ca. 60 metres shorter than planned). Breakwater completed.

1886

August, breakwater damaged in storm; repaired and strengthened 1887–89.

1891

Ferry service to Dunedin ceased.

1894

23 May, Cape Wanbrow lighthouse fitted with a new occulting light purchased from Melbourne, range 15 miles.

1901

Additional piles driven to strengthen Sumpter Wharf.

1906

Holmes Wharf commenced by Fitzgerald & Bignell. New northern end fitted during upgrade to Sumpter Wharf. 18 August, fire destroyed a small wooden building near Sumpter Wharf used by Railways as a lamp-room.

1907
Holmes Wharf completed on the North Mole. Initial 152 m middle section of wharf and a dolphin at the eastern end.

1908
Wharf shed and flagstaff erected on Holmes Wharf.

1909
Watersiders' shelter built on Holmes Wharf.

1911
Progress converted to a stationary dredge by Stephenson & Cook; 1 March, 4.9 m light staff at end of the breakwater replaced by a 7.9 m lattice tower.

1913
Training piles placed between Holmes Wharf and the eastern dolphin. New flagstaff erected on Holmes Wharf.

1916–17
Seawall between Sumpter Wharf and the SE corner of the harbour pitched to a regular grade, new posts and handrails erected and a permanent footpath erected. 1917 more piles added to Sumpter Wharf. *Progress* sold for conversion to a trading vessel.

1918–19
Seawall extensions built between Sumpter Wharf and Normanby Wharf, handrails erected etc.

1920
Wharves lit by electricity.

1921
Foreshore Improvements Committee (later the Friendly Bay Improvement Society Inc and later still the Oamaru Carnival Society Inc) formed.

1922
Battened piles driven on the eastern side of the Sumpter Wharf curved viaduct to strengthen it; Holmes Wharf dolphin extended. Friendly Bay named.

1922–29
Western reclamation built up, levelled and seawall, footpaths and road (transferred to the Oamaru Borough Council in 1927) tidied up. Land leased to oil companies, who erected storage tanks: British Oil Co (1925), Vacuum Oil Co (1926) and Texas Co (1929).

1924
Watersiders' waiting room erected on Holmes Wharf.

1925
Lighthouse converted from oil lamp to electricity.

1928–29
Holmes Wharf lengthened, strengthened and equipped with electric capstans and bollards.

1934
A new rope shed, incorporating an office for the harbourmaster, built on Holmes Wharf (old rope shed near the breakwater demolished). Marine Department approved improving rail access at the landward end of Holmes Wharf and realigning the landing stage parallel with the wharf.

1936
197.5 m landward end section of the breakwater raised by 2.1 m; first stone deposited on the Ramsay Extension.

1938–39
Southern end of Sumpter Wharf widened to improve railway access. Similar improvements made to Holmes Wharf.

1940
New launch slipway completed on the west side of Normanby Wharf; 2–7 November, visit by the last Home boat, the *Somerset*.

1941–42
North Mole widened and strengthened to enable buildings to be removed from Holmes Wharf; 1943 new hut built for police.

1943
G.W. Todd permitted to build a fish shed on Normanby Wharf; 15 November, Frederick Maynard and Allan McIntosh killed in quarry blast accident.

1944
Ramsay Extension sealed off; subsequently deteriorated. 4 February, Cape Wanbrow lighthouse lit from a new concrete tower, automated, acetone acetylene; 18 March, *Kakapo* touched while leaving port, sparking an internal row within the harbour board.

1945
5 March, Cape Wanbrow lighthouse first lit by electricity.

1946
15 July, frigate HMS *Whitehead Bay* pays the last visit to Oamaru by a Royal Navy warship.

1947–48
NOY&PBC given permission to renovate and use the old pre-World War I dredging jetty off the Foreshore Road.

1948
1 December; two ratings from HMNZS *Bellona* killed in a boating accident off the harbour; 2 December, *Turakina* memorial unveiled.

1949
Landing built for fishermen on Sumpter Wharf.

1951
March–May, waterfront lockout.

1952
NOY&PBC slipway completed off Breakwater Road. OHB pays off its 1911 debt reconsolidation.

1953
New watersiders' rest rooms built alongside the rope shed on the North Mole. Shell Oil completed oil tanks for use of the coastal tanker *Tanea* (arrived 9 December).

1955
16 May, *Hotunui* begins regular services from Oamaru for the Northern Steam Ship Co.

1956
Dolphin at end of Holmes Wharf, damaged by *Kauri* in 1953 demolished and rebuilt.

1957
First tetrapods placed on the breakwater; BP oil installation completed.

1958
Breakwater raised for a further 68 m; old Cape Wanbrow lighthouse residence demolished.

1962
Small area of land north of Holmes Wharf reclaimed.

1963
October, *Awanui* trials unloading of palletised cargo direct on to trucks.

1964
March, *Tanea* ceased calling; oil pipeline removed 1966 as part of Holmes Wharf upgrade.

1966
17 January, Oamaru ceased to be a port of entry. 21 December, major blast in the quarry brings down 60,000 tonnes of rock; dredge *W.H. Orbell* carried out a major dredging programme; Holmes Wharf upgrade began with the removal of the oil pipeline and the demolition of the rowing club building.

1967
$180,000 loan raised to reconstruct Holmes Wharf (work completed 1971); the *Calm* loaded the first shipment of bulk grain; slipway rebuilt.

1968
New slipway constructed.

1973
August, The last trans-Tasman ship (*Koraki*) sailed from Oamaru.

1974
14 May, The coaster *Holmdale* was the last ship to use the Port of Oamaru.

1975
August, Oamaru watersiders declared redundant. Port officially closed to shipping.

1976
March, fish container and small crane placed on Holmes Wharf.

1978
31 March, Oamaru Harbour Board abolished. Administration taken over by Oamaru Borough Council and managed through the Oamaru Harbour Committee (with representation from the Waitaki and Waimate County Councils).

1982
Turakina memorial removed from Friendly Bay to make room for planned cement silo; later re-erected on Lookout Point

1986
Boat compound opened in part of the harbour quarry, and Normanby Wharf slipway repaired.

1988
Jetties completed by the NOY&PBC slipway.

1989
Waitaki District Council (WDC) formed from merger of the Oamaru Borough and the Waitaki County Councils.

1991
Slipway rebuilt, de Geests complete breakwater repair contract abandoned by John Cradock in 1990.

1992
Oamaru Blue Penguin Colony opened in the former harbour quarry.

1993
WDC officially named the right-of-way Breakwater Road.

1995
Cape Wanbrow lighthouse disestablished.

1997
Harbour entrance dredged for the first time since 1971.

2003
WDC chief executive resigns over failed 2001 breakwater repairs.

2005
Holmes Wharf dolphin demolished. H2O restaurant opened on the Cross Wharf.

2006
22 May, Penguin colony visitor centre enlarged. Tetrapod construction resumed.

2007
Contractors constructed a road on the inside of the breakwater to facilitate repairs.

Appendix 2

Wrecks and accidents

This is a list of major casualties to trading vessels and fishing boats.
For more information on vessels not discussed in the main text of this book, see Bruce Collins, *Rocks, Reefs and Sandbars: A History of Otago Shipwrecks*, Otago Heritage Books, Dunedin, 1995, C.W.N. Ingram, *New Zealand Shipwrecks* (8th edition, edited by Edith Diggle, Lynton Diggle and Keith Gordon), Hodder Moa, Auckland, 2007, and Gavin McLean, *Oamaru Harbour: Port in a Storm*, Dunmore Press, Palmerston North, 1982.

1860

October	*Oamaru Lass*	schooner	28 tons. Stranded; vessel advertised for sale November, recovered and renamed *Nora*.

1862

3 March	*Wellington*	schooner	54 tons. Broke anchor cable and drifted ashore, becoming a total loss. Uninsured
6 March	*Star of Tasmania*	schooner	31 tons. Stranded in heavy surf; refloated.
5 April	*Robert and Betsy*	brigantine	383 tons. Parted cable and drifted ashore. Wreck bought for £10. Foremast preserved by harbour slipway 1990s.
29 September	*Brisk*	schooner	15 tons. Hit reef off Cape Wanbrow, but recovered without difficulty.

1865

13 March	*Gazehound*	barque	383 tons. Total wreck after breaking cables in calm conditions.

1867

13 March	*Vixen*	schooner	17 tons. Wrecked in heavy seas but later refloated. See pp. 23, 25.
13 March	*Stately*	schooner	86 tons. Total wreck south of the landing place. See p. 25.
31 July	*Midlothian*	ketch	15 tons. Refloated 21 August.
31 July	*Hope*	cutter	See pp. 25, 27.
31 July	*Vistula*	brigantine	See pp. 25–26.
14 August	*Banshee*	schooner	70 tons. See p. 27.
23 November	*Highlander*	brig	195 tons. Total wreck. See p. 28.
24 November	*Caroline*	schooner	38 tons. Left the anchorage, but beached after sails split.

1868

3 February	*Star of Tasmania*	ship	623 tons. Total wreck. Four lives lost. See pp. 29–31.
3 February	*Water Nymph*	ship	548 tons. Total wreck. See pp. 29–31.
3 February	*Otago*	ketch	26 tons. Total wreck. See pp. 29, 31.
24 March	*Fly*	cutter	15 tons. Total wreck after drifting ashore; vessel's timbers were rotten.

1869

12 June	*Cora*	schooner	46 tons. Stranded 12 June 1869 below the flagstaff. 24 June moved 0.6 metre feet by an earthquake. Refloated 9 July.

1871

31 July	*Premier*	barque	296 tons. Went ashore just west of the wrecked jetty; refloated 29 September, but again caught in a storm and driven ashore.

1872

24 February	*Onehunga*	schooner	61 tons. Driven ashore after failing to put to sea; several salvage attempts failed and she eventually broke up.
28 July	*Our Hope*	brig	237 tons. Dragged her anchor in a NE gale and wrecked; crew rescued by the rocket brigade.

1873

6 May	*Mary Ogilvie*	schooner	72 tons. Abandoned to underwriters but refloated 27 May.
10 May	*Margaret Campbell*	three-masted schooner	122 tons. Driven ashore near the lagoon, where she quickly broke up.
28 August	*Emile*	brig	214 tons. Unable to proceed to sea after being hot by the schooner *Jane Anderson* and went ashore without loss of life.
28 August	*Scotsman*	brig	231 tons. Wrecked in stormy weather.
17 September	*Oriti*	schooner	67 tons. Sometimes spelled *Oreti*. Relaunched 30 September (narrowly escaped grounding again).
28 September	*Jane*	cutter	Lost wind while moving berths inside the breakwater, cables snapped and went ashore. Refloated, damaged, that night with the assistance of the landing service boatmen.

1874

2 May	*Ocean Wave*	three-masted schooner	118 tons. Wrecked in heavy seas; crew rescued by the rocket brigade.
2 May	*Emulous*	brigantine	157 tons. Stranded without loss of life; three times refloated, only to strand again. 11 October refloated for a fourth time and got within eight miles of Port Chalmers, only to be forced back to Oamaru, where she stranded five miles north of the town.
28 September	*Richard and Mary*	schooner	44 tons. Missed stays. Relaunched 21 October on the second attempt.
3 October	*United Brothers*	schooner	50 tons. Beached after developing a leak and broke up; hull decayed.

1875

13 February	*Fanny*	ketch	25 tons, Parted cable, missed stays, hit breakwater and run ashore. Refloated 15 February.
8 May	*Elderslie*	schooner	203 tons, Fouled schooner *Young Dick* while attempting to leave port in heavy seas and wrecked near site of Sumpter Wharf.

1879

17 June	*Franklin Belle*	ketch	30 tons. Run ashore by the lagoon after breaking adrift in heavy seas. See p. 46.

1883

31 March	*Friendship*	schooner	53 tons, being used as a fishing vessel. Total wreck after heavy seas carried away her rudder while entering port

1895
8 December   *Fifeshire*   steamer   Grounded off Cape Wanbrow. Refloated and escorted by tug to Lyttelton

1956
29 July   *Julia*   fishing boat   11 metres. Sank alongside Holmes Wharf after the stopcock in an intake valve was left open; salvaged 30/31 July.

1960
7 February   *Joyce*   fishing boat   10.1 metres. Wrecked north of the port after the skipper fell asleep.

1972
2 May   *Orion*   fishing boat   12.2 metres. This Timaru boat capsized while hauling in the catch 35 km NE of Oamaru.

1973
9 January   *Seawitch*   fishing boat   13.4 metres. Fouled propeller and ran aground opposite the railway station; refloated successfully.

1974
August   *Edie*   fishing boat   9.1 metres. Sunk when heavy waves swept a shed off Holmes Wharf, sinking the boat; salvaged and rebuilt as a pleasure craft.

25/26 June   *Otago*   fishing boat   Sank alongside Sumpter Wharf during the night, refloated next day.

1994
21 April   *Waitaki*   fishing boat   11.3 metres. Run aground to prevent sinking.

1999
25 February   *Edie*   pleasure boat   Run aground to prevent sinking; recovered.

2002
11 January   *Eleanor*   fishing boat   Beached in a sinking condition; recovered.

2003
21 January   *Moana*   fishing boat   9.8 metres. Sank north of Kakanui, drowning the crewman. Recovered May 2004. See pp. 124–25.

2004
12 August   *Waitaki*   pleasure craft   11.3 metres. Former fishing boat. Sank at moorings; refloated next day. See p 126.

The Waiwera *and a cabbage tree frame this view while fishing launches occupy the foreground.*

– North Otago Museum 1977

Notes

Abbreviations

ANZ – Archives New Zealand
ATL – Alexander Turnbull Library
NOT – North Otago Museum
ODT – *Otago Daily Times*
OHB – Oamaru Harbour Board
OM – *Oamaru Mail*
OT&WR – *Oamaru Times and Waitaki Reporter* (*North Otago Times* from 1870)
OW – *Otago Witness*

Overture

1 Kenneth Cumberland, *Landmarks*, Reader's Digest Services, Surry Hills, 1981, p. 255.

Chapter One

1 This comment was on a map of Ohimaraí produced in 1841–42 for E. Halswell. See K.C. McDonald, *White Stone Country*, p. 26.
2 K.C. McDonald, *Oamaru 1878: A Colonial Town*, p. 21.
3 A.W. Reed, *The Reed Dictionary of New Zealand Place Names*, 2002 edition, Reed Books, Auckland, p. 350.
4 Reg Graham and R.G. Lister, *Where Land Meets Sea*, John McIndoe, Dunedin, 1969, introduction (unpaginated).
5 Janet Frame, *The Edge of the Alphabet, Faces in the Water and The Edge of the Alphabet*, Vintage, Auckland, 2005, p. 375.
6 Kirk Hargreaves, *On the Next Tide: Portraits and Anecdotes of New Zealand Fishermen and Women*, Canterbury University Press, Christchurch, 1998, p. 22
7 John Darby, R. Ewan Fordyce, Alan Mark, Keith Probert, Colin Townsend (eds), *The Natural History of Southern New Zealand*, University of Otago Press, Dunedin, 2003, p. 271.
8 *ibid.*, p. 278.
9 Ian Church, *Opening the Manifest on Otago's Infant Years: Shipping Arrivals and Departures, Otago Harbour and Coast 1770–1860*, Otago Heritage Books, Dunedin, 2002, p. 165.
10 *NOT*, 19 Se 1879.
11 *OW*, 30 Apr 1859.
12 *History of North Otago*, p. 45.
13 *The Boy-Colonists: Or, Eight Years of Colonial Life in Otago, New Zealand*, Simpkin, Marshall & Co, London and Thos Shrimpton & Son, Oxford, 1878, pp. 30-1.
14 *OT&WR*, 14 October 1870.
15 *ibid.*, 8 Oct 1869.

16 *ibid.*, 8 Oct 1869.
17 *ibid.*, 9 Nov 1866.
18 *ibid.*, 5 Apr 1867.
19 *ibid.*, 22 Mar 1867.
20 *ibid.*, 19 Mar 1867.
21 William Thomson, Harbour Report, Departmental Reports, 1866, *Otago Votes and Proceedings 1866–9*, p.34.
22 *OT&WR*, 2 Aug 1867.
23 *ibid.*, 20 Aug 1867.
24 *ibid.*, 1 Oct 1867.
25 *ibid.*, 29 Oct 1867.
26 *ibid.*, 5 Nov 1867.
27 *ibid.*, 26 Nov 1867.
28 *ibid.*, 8 Feb 1868.

Chapter Two

1 *OT&WR*, 20 Dec 1867.
2 *ibid.*, 10 Dec 1867
3 William Thomson, Harbour Report, Departmental Reports, 1866, *Otago Votes and Proceedings 1866–9*, p.32.
4 *ibid.*, 1868, p. 22.
5 *ibid..*, p. 44.
6 *OT&WR*, 31 Aug 1869.
7 *ibid.*, 26 Oct 1869. The brigade met for the first time on 1 November at the Northern Hotel.
8 *ibid.*, 28 Jan 1870.
9 William Sewell, report 24 Mar 1874, Departmental Reports, 1866, *Otago Votes and Proceedings1872–4*, p. 89.
10 Two preceding pages based on Dobson and Blackett's report, 16 Jan 1869, *Otago Votes & Proceedings 1869*, pp. 4–6.
11 *OT&WR*, 28 Sep 1869.
12 The machinery commenced work on 20 April. It consists of a revolving drum with beaters which, on the shingle and cement being thrown into a hopper, under a stream of water poured from a hose, thoroughly mix the ingredients of the blocks. *Oamaru Times*, 21 April 1871. Eight days later the *Nelson Examiner and New Zealand Chronicle* reported that the first five blocks of concrete have been moulded by the contractor, Mr Walkem, on the shi[n]gle bank near the lagoon. This suggests that at least some early blocks were also manufactured on the proposed dock site.
13 *NOT*, 3 Feb 1871.
14 *ibid.*, 2 Aug 1870.
15 *ibid.*, 12 Sep 1871.
16 Thomas Forrester to James Blackett, 18 Sep 1886, M1, 4/3082, Oamaru Harbour Works Correspondence, ANZ.
17 *OW*, 21 Jun 1873.
18 *NOT*, 3 Aug 1873.
19 *Evening Star*, quoted in *NOT*, 14 Mar 1873.

20 *NOT*, 15 Sep 1874.
21 *NOT*, 6 May 1875.
22 *ibid.*, 19 Nov 1872.
23 *ibid.*, 12 Feb 1881.
24 K.C. McDonald, *White Stone Country*, p. 141.
25 *Otago Guardian*, 23 Dec 1873.
26 The cottages were demolished by the Benevolent Trustees over the summer of 1905/06.
27 *NOT*, 28 Jan 1879.
28 *ibid.*, 4 and 14 October 1876.
29 *ibid.*, 7 Sep 1878.
30 *ibid.*, 30 May 1884.
31 Log of the schooner *Swordfish* from Hobart for Oamaru, Micro-MS-733, ATL.
32 Helen Beaglehole, *Lighting the Coast: A History of New Zealand's Coastal Lighthouse System*, Canterbury University Press, Christchurch, 2006, p. 86.
33 The Lighthouses of New Zealand, Fabian Bell, *Otago Witness*, 13 Feb 1901.
34 *ibid.*, 18 Jan 1881.
35 *NOT*, 14 Jun 1879.
36 Rollo Arnold, *New Zealand's Burning: The Settlers World in the Mid 1880s*, Victoria University Press, Wellington, 1994, p. 213.
37 K.C. McDonald, *Oamaru 1878: A Colonial Town*, 1878 Publication Group of the Waitaki District Council, Oamaru, 2006, p. 67.
38 *NOT*, 9 Dec 1882.
39 OM, 3 Sep 1884.
40 *ibid.*, 5 Jan 1884.
41 *ibid.*, 26 February 1884.
42 *ibid.*, 7 Jul 1884.
43 NOT, 8 Sep 1884.
44 *ibid.*, 18 and 19 Aug 1884.
45 OM, 6 Sep 1884.
46 *ibid.*, 25 Sep 1884.
47 *ibid.*, 14 Oct 1884

Chapter Three

1 *Beginnings*, p. 120.
2 *NOT*, 15 Dec 1882.
3 *ibid.*, 17 Jan 1888.
4 *ibid.*, 19 May 1890.
5 *ibid.*, 24 Feb 1891.
6 *ibid.*, 12 Jan 892.
7 *ibid.*, 23 Feb 1875.
8 *ibid.*, 11 Nov 1897.
9 Thomas Forrester to James Blackett, 18 Sep 1884, M1, 4/3082, Oamaru Harbour Works Correspondence, ANZ.
10 *NOT*, 28 Mar 1885.
11 *OW*, 30 Apr 1886.
12 Ian McGibbon, *The Path to Gallipoli: Defending New Zealand 1840–1915*, GP

Books, Wellington, 1991, p. 47.
13 Peter Cooke, *Defending New Zealand: Ramparts on the Sea 1840–1950s*, Defence of New Zealand Study Group, Wellington, 4th impression, 2001, p.140.
14 *OM*, 16 and 19 Dec 1884. According to *Defending New Zealand*, the unit became the Oamaru Rifle Volunteers in October 1895.
15 *OW*, 30 Apr 1886.
16 *ibid*.
17 *Timaru Herald*, 26 Apr 1886.
18 *ibid*., 10 Dec 1886.
19 *ibid*., 27 Jan 1888.
20 OHB AR 1889.
21 *OW*, 6 Nov 1890.
22 *Southland Times*, 25 Oct 1889.
23 *Evening Post*, 13 Aug 1891.
24 *ibid*., 22 Oct 1891.
25 *NOT*, Dec 10 1900.
26 J.C. Voss, *Venturesome Voyages*, Grafton Books, London, 1989, p. 155.
27 *ibid*., p. 60.
28 *NOT*, 28 Feb 1903.
29 OHB harbour master's letterbook, 23 Dec 1895, NOM.
30 *ibid*., 19 Jan 1895.
31 *ibid*., 6 Jun 1903.
32 *ibid*., 10 Jun 1907.

Chapter Four
1 *OW*, 5 Feb 1908.
2 *ibid*., 11 Mar 1908.
3 *ibid*., 3 Jun 1908.
4 *ibid*., 8 Jan 1908
5 *ibid*., 30 Dec 1908.
6 *ibid*., 3 Apr 1907.
7 *Evening Post*, 9 Sep 1910.
8 Report of Cyrus W. Williams, 25 Jul 1914, NOM.
9 Furkert, report, *OM*, 12 Sep 1933.
10 *ibid*.
11 OHB minutes, 8 Aug 1933, NOM.
12 *OM*, 9 Oct 1923.
13 Marine Engineer to Secretary of Marine, 17 Nov 1938, ABPL 7457 Acc W4932 43/9/9/2 Part 1, Sumpter Wharf, ANZ.

Chapter Five
1 Peter Cooke, *Defending New Zealand: Ramparts on the Sea 1840–1950s*, Defence of New Zealand Study Group, Wellington 4th impressin, 2001, pp. 489–90.
2 *Oamaru Mail*, 7 Nov 1950.
3 *ibid*., 22 Oct 1949.
4 *ibid*., 1 Feb 1955.
5 *ibid*., 1 Jun 1943.
6 *ibid*., 27 Mar 1943.
7 Memo to acting minister of finance, 9 Mar 1943, AALR 873 Acc W3158 10 T53/182, ANZ.
8 Oamaru Rowing Club (inc), *100 Years 1886–1986:Centennial Booklet*, Oamaru, 1986, p. 31.
9 http://www.nzhistory.net.nz/politics/the-1951-waterfront-dispute.

10 *ODT*, 16 Feb 1951.
11 *ibid*., 9 Mar 1951.
12 *ibid*., 14 May 1951.
13 James Revelley, *Registering Interest: Waterfront Labour Relations in New Zealand, 1953 to 2000*, Research in Maritime History No. 25, International Maritime Economic History Association, St John's, 2003, p. 8.
14 Quoted in Peter Cooke, *Shell in New Zealand*, Shell Heritage Society, Wellington, 2004, p. 129.
15 Henry Williams, deposition, 24 Nov 1959, AAPR, Acc W3282, 10, 13/28659, Part 2, ANZ.
16 Henry Williams, statement, AAPR, Acc 3350, 10, ANZ.
17 J.C. Winders to secretary of marine, AAPR, Acc W3282, 10, 13/2860, part 2, ANZ.
18 Allan McKay, deposition, 2 Dec 1959, AAPR, Acc 3350, 10, ANZ.
19 Rowland Masterman, deposition, M1, 12/1113.
20 J.D. Carrick, evidence, AAPR, Acc 3350, 10, ANZ.
21 Cosmo Keith, evidence, AAPR, Acc 3350, 10, ANZ.
22 E.F. Rainbow to minister of marine, 30 Mar 1960, M1, 12/113, ANZ.
23 *OM*, 16 Mar 1961.
24 NSSCo to OHB, 16 May and 10 Jun 1955, Northern Steam Ship Co file, OHB letter file 326/71e, NOM.
25 Chairman's report, OHB annual report, NOM.
26 Various letters from masters and agents, Harbourmaster's correspondence 1956–74, 1963–5, OHB letter file 302/71b, NOM.
27 *Evening Post*, 23 Nov 1963.
28 OHB minutes, 4 Sep 1973, NOM.
29 http://www.nzcoastalshipping.com/mv%20holmdale.html

Chapter Six
1 *Oamaru Mail*, 10 June 1983.
2 A.A. Bird to Hon. W. Freer. 25 July 1973, OHB Letterbook 1970-4, NOM.
3 Stephen L. Bloxham, *A Brief History of the Oamaru Harbour Board 1874-1978*, Oamaru Harbour Board, Oamaru, 1978, unpaginated.
4 *AJHR*, Report of Ministry of Transport for the Year Ended 31 March 1984, F.5, p. 15.
5 Harry Morton, Carol Johnston and Barbara Chinn, *The Cornerstone Century: The Story of Milburn New Zealand Limited*, New Zealand Cement Holdings Ltd, Christchurch, 2002, p. 119.
6 Bloxham, *A Brief History*.
7 Capt A. Grieve to Nautical Adviser, 9 Oct 1975, Ministry of Transport ABPL 7457 W5222 7 46/3/20, Aids to Navigation: Oamaru Harbour, ANZ.
8 W. Owen, monthly reports, 1975–77, OHB leter files, 361/72 a, NOM.

9 Grieve to J. Rudhall, 27 Jan 1987, ABPL 7457 W5222 7 46/3/20, Aids to Navigation: Oamaru Harbour, ANZ
10 Capt A. Grieve to Gavin McLean, 6 Nov 2007.
11 *ibid*.
12 Grieve to Rudhall, 6 May 1987, ABPL 7457 W5222 7 46/3/20, ANZ.
13 File Note, Nautical Adviser to Legal Section, ABPL 7457 W5222 7 46/3/20, Aids to Navigation: Oamaru Harbour, ANZ.
14 *Oamaru Mail*, 10 Mar 1986.
15 Lawrence Hardy, interview with Gavin McLean, 6 Dec 2007.
16 Kirk Hargreaves, *On the Next Tide: Portraits and Anecdotes of New Zealand Fishermen and Women*, Canterbury University Press, Christchurch, 1998, p. 22.
17 *Oamaru Mail*, 18 Dec 1991.
18 *ibid*., p. 23.
19 *ODT*, 10, 14, 18, 25, 29 May and 5 and 8 Oct 1996.
20 *Timaru Herald*, 19 Dec 2003.
21 *ODT*, 24 March 2004.
22 *ibid*., 26 Aug, 2006.
23 *OM*, 12 Jun 2006.
24 *ODT*, 20 May 2006.
25 *ibid*., 23 Feb 2004.
26 *ibid*., 21 March 2007.
27 Robyn Flynn, Project Coordinator, Holcim to Gavin McLean, 5 Dec 2007.

Envoi
1 Sheila Leaver-Cooper (Ian S. Smith, photographs), *Janet Frame's Kingdom by the Sea: Oamaru*, Lincoln University Press with Daphne Brasell Associates Ltd, Lincoln, 1997, p. 53.
2 http://www.doc.govt.nz/templates/page.aspx?id=39116
3 http://www.nzherald.co.nz/topic/story.cfm?c_id=350&objectid=10444559
4 *The Waitaki Link*, WDC, Aug 2007, p. 3. In April 2007 CHImp member Ken Mitchell presented the council with a report on his study of UK maritime and industrial heritage sites.
5 Allan Cubitt, Decision of Commissioner December 2006 in the Matter of: Resource Consent Application LRC06/08 by Cormorants on Waterfront (N. & J. de Geest), Dunedin, December 2006. He granted consent subject to covenants banning domestic pets potentially harmful to penguins and the right to complain about the operation, and any associated effects, of the adjacent railway, road or port.
6 *ODT*, 22 Feb 2005.
7 *ibid*., 17 Mar 2005.
8 James Belich, *Making Peoples, A History of the New Zealanders From Polynesian Settlement to the End of the Nineteenth Century*, Allen Lane, Auckland, 1996, p. 450.

Index

Adams, Lorraine, 131
Aitken, Henry, 46
Antarctic exploration, 84
Arnold, Rollo, 49
Ashcroft, James, 33
Atkinson, Edward, 84
Aubrey, C., 64

Cabot, Captain Edwin, 31
Bain, Captain E.,
Baker family, 30–31
Balfour, David, 38
Balfour, J.M., 25, 48
Barber, Nick, 136
Barr, George, 37–38
Bathgate, John, 33
Beattie, Herries, 17
Bee, William, 57
Berry, George 125
Bird, A.A., 120
Blackett, John, 37
Blair, J., 82
Borrie, Donald, 79
Bouman, Captain Herman, 23
Bourke, Captain Edmund, 58
Bowers, 'Birdie', 84
breakwater: campaign for and against, 31–2,
    37; construction, 38–42, 44–45, 49;
    damage and repairs, 60–61, 98–99, 123,
    126–28; extensions, 90–92; Ramsay
    Extension, 90–92, 98–99, 119, 123,
    127–28, 140
Breen, Leo, 123
Briscoe & Co, 49
Brookes, William, 29

Calder, Hugh, 25
Campbell, John, 120
Cautley, Colonel Henry, 64
Cherry-Garrard, Apsley, 84
CHImp (Culture and Heritage
    Implementation Group), 134
Coastal erosion, 16–18, 126–27
Collett, Brian, 100
Criterion Hotel, 57, 135
Cross, A.F., 85
Culbert, William, 29–30
Cumberland, Kenneth, 8
Customs service, 139

Daniel Smith Industries, 126
Darbyshire, G.A.K., 82
Delmer, Captain, 47
Denny, Reg, 117
Department of Conservation, 131–32, 134
Dobson, Edward, 37
dredges and dredging, 49, 52–53, 60; 79, 93,
    107, 109, 111, 123, 125–26; see also
    individual dredges

Edie, Captain, 24, 45
Elwell, E. Simeon, 20–1
Elworthy, Jonathan, 117
E.R Garden & Partners, 118–19
Evans, Edward, 84

Evans, P., 59

Fernando-Armesto, Felipe, 57
fishing (commercial), 85, 92; 118, 121–25,
    140, recreational, 92
fishing boats: *Aorere*, 2; *Clan Cameron*, 122;
    Edie, 120, 144; *Eleanor*, 144; *Enterprise*,
    122–23; *Joyce*, 144; *Julia*, 144; *Moana*,
    124–25, 144; *Orion*, 144; *Otago*, 144;
    Seawitch, 144; *South Wind*, 120; *Time Out*,
    124; *Toroa*, 8; *Venture*, 105; *Waitaki*, 124,
    144
Fitzgerald & Bignell, 73
flagstaff/signal station, 28–31, 34
Fodor, G.F., 65
Forrester, Thomas, 7, 39, 40, 49, 52, 61, 82,
    139
Frame, Janet, 18
France, Henry, 27
Friendly Bay, 9, 83, 92–3, 101, 131
Friendly Bay Improvement Committee (later
    FBI Society, and later still the Oamaru
    Carnival Society[Inc]), 92, 131, 137
Foreshore Improvement Committee, 92
Furkert, F.W., 90–91

Gair, George, 118
Gallagher, John, 100
Gilchrist, J., 73
Gillies, G.T., 99, 119
Grave, E., 57
Graves Walkway, 133, 136
Grenfell, G.L., 20
Grey, Sir George, 55
Grieve, Captain Alex, 105, 120–1, 131
Guthrie, T.C.C., 52

Hancox, Captain John, 104, 120
Hansby, Captain, 63–64
Harbour 2 Ocean Restaurant, 135–36
Harbourside Implementation Group, 137
Hardy, Lawrence, 121
Hardy, Tom, 20
Hassell, James, 20, 46
Hay, William, 20
Hesketh, Alfred, 42
Hessewood, Keith, 100
Hertslett, H.C., 19
Hilmann, T., 58
Historic Places Trust, New Zealand, 133,
    136
Holcim (New Zealand) Ltd, *see* New
    Zealand Cement Holdings Ltd
Holm Shipping Co. 83, 105, 108
Holmes, James, 73

Jones, Joseph, 41
John Mill & Co, 77
Johnson, Captain Robert, 48

Kakanui, 34
Kincaid and McQueen, 39–40

La Roche, C.A., 82,
Lake, James, 76–77
lagoon, 18, 34, 36–37, 46

landing service, 19–22, 42
Lane, Edward, 59, 85
Laney, Bill, 101
Lee, G.A., 91
lighthouses, Cape Wanbrow, 48, 139, 141
Local Government Commission, 120
Logan, Mick, 100
Lothian, J., 82
Luxton, Kenny, 70

Macandrew, James, 38
MacLean, Captain Jim, 120
McDonald, K.C., 49
McGregor, John, 37–38, 52, 60, 90
McIntosh, Allan, 140
McKay, Allan, 105
McKenzie, George, 31
McKinnon, Neil, 84
McLean, Joan, 101
McLean, Murray, 101
McLellan, John, 122, 124
McLelland, A.C., 99
Mantel, W.B., 17
Maritime Safety Authority, 125
Matheson, Captain Henry, 46
Maynard, Frederick, 140
Meehan, John, 84
Miller, David, 66
Miller, John, 66
Miller & Smillie, 46
Milligan, Robert, 79–80, 82, 85
Mills, James, 45
Ministry of Transport, 120–1
Mitchell, J.H., 120
Mitchell, Ken, 127
'Moa' [steam crane], 39, 62
Moeraki, 18, 25, 33–34, 48
Monson, R.W., 79
Morrison, Alexander, 79

newspapers: *Evening Post*, 69, 82, 109;
    Evening Star, 41; *Financial Times*, 69;
    Oamaru Mail, 60, 83, 85, 92, 117;
    Oamaru Times and Waitaki Reporter [later
    North Otago Times], 22, 24–25, 28, 33,
    38, 41, 46, 49, 69, 72; *Otago Daily Times*,
    103; *Otago Witness*, 12, 20, 41, 65, 77–78;
    Timaru Herald, 55; *Waikato Times*, 41
New Zealand Cement Holdings Ltd (later
    Holcim [New Zealand Ltd]), 117–19, 128
New Zealand Ports Authority, 117–18
New Zealand Shipping Co, 52, 71–72, 88
Nicholls, Jasper, 79
Normanby, Lord, 43, 46
Northern Hotel, 21–22; 26, 33, 56
Northern Steam Ship Co, 109, 141
North Mole, 46, 48, 121, 139
North Otago Yacht and Power Boat Club,
    10, 100, 119–120, 140

Oamaru: Maori history, 17–18; origins of
    name, 17; coastal erosion 16–18; seabed,
    18; impact of inadequate port facilities on
    economy of, 33–34; switch from dock

option to deepwater port, 38–39; celebration of export port status; 55; social use of harbour, 58–60; Antarctic connection, 84; heritage, 133–135
Oamaru Artillery Volunteers, 64
Oamaru Blue Penguin Colony, 131–33, 141
Oamaru Boating Club (formerly Oamaru Yachting Club), 59;
Oamaru Borough Council, 120, 123, 140
Oamaru Creek, 18
Oamaru Dock Trust, 37–38, 139
Oamaru and Dunedin Steam Ship Co, 45
Oamaru Harbour: immigration trades/barracks, 42, 44; impact of Victorian railway competition on, 49; export frozen meat trade, 49–55; competition with Timaru, 55; social life, 57–58; mock bombardment (1885), 63–65; defence, 63–65, 97; industrial relations, 66–67, 101–104; pilot service, 69; South African War grain boom, 69–72; excursion trade, 80–81; World War I, 82–83; pollution, 92–93; loss of overseas trade, 97–99; oil trade, 103–4; railways competition 1960s/70s, 109–10; oil exploration, 114–15; closure, 115; cement port plans, 116–19; post-closure decay 130–31; penguin colony 131–32; heritage and tourism, 134–37; see also breakwater, flagstaff and signal station, lighthouses and wharves and structures
Oamaru Harbour Board: formation, 42, 139; fixed final size of the port, 46, 48; Financial difficulties, 67–69, 77–79, 82; Otematata estate, 67; disagreement over replacement of the Progress, 77–79, 82; breakwater extension debates, 89–92; post-World War II internal disagreements, 99; centennial 119–120; abolition, 120; buildings: harbour board offices, 6–7; watchman's hut/signalman's hut, 28–29, 31
Oamaru Harbour Board Loan Act 1908, 79
Oamaru Harbour Committee, 120–23
Oamaru Landing Service Co, 31
Oamaru Naval Artillery Volunteers Unit, 58, 64
Oamaru Rocket Brigade, 34–35, 139
Oamaru Rowing Club (formerly Oamaru Boating Club), 100–101
Oamaru Union Rowing Club, 59
Oamaru Whitestone Civic Trust, 133, 136–37
Oates, L.E., 84
Opus International Consultants Ltd, 127
Otago Provincial Government, 19–20, 33, 139
Overseas Shipowners' Allotment Committee, 83–84, 97–98
Owen, Bill, 121

Pallant, Captain Joseph, 61
Paterson, W.H., 82
Patterson, Captain D.R., 104
Patterson, George, 101
Paton, Captain, 26
Peach, Frank, 82
Pennell, Lieutenant Harry, 84
Perham, Glen, 125
Petrie, David, 29
Philp & Jones, 53

pleasure craft, see recreational boating
Port Otago Ltd, 125
Portside Restaurant and Bar, 136
Preston, Dean, 134
Public Works Department, 97
Pulman, Douglas, 101

Quarry, harbour, 46–48, 98, 140

Railways; impact of the South Island Main Trunk on coastal shipping, 49, 78; Wansbeck Street pedestrian overbridge, 73; rail ferry/freight forwarder competition with coastal shipping, 109, 113; and the Weston cement plant, 118, 128
Railway Boating Club, 59
Rainbow, Captain, E.F., 105
Ramsay, Captain James, 72, 82, 84
Ramsay Extension, see breakwater
recreational boating: coracle racing, 134; rowing, 58, 92; yachting 10, 58, 99. Individual yachts/launches: Aid, 59; Kakanui, 59; Leader, 92; Lily, 92; Lyric, 10; Maggie, 59; Maori Chief, 59; Pinafore, 59; Rose, 59; Tilikum, 70; Wild Rose, 59; see also specific clubs
Reid, John, 52–53, 79
Richardson & Co., 108
Robertson, Russell 'Rusty', 100–01
Robison, Hugh, 18
Rose, W.H., 79, 82
Ross, David, 42
Roxby, Eustace, 20
Rudhall, J., 121

Sailing Alone Around the World, 70
Sanford Ltd, 122, 124–25
Scott, Rear-admiral A.E., 65
Scott, Captain Robert Falcon, 12, 84
Scott's Own Sea Scouts, 93, 136
Seawalls, 131, 140
Sewell, Captain William, 20, 23, 29, 34, 46, 72, 82
Shadbolt, Maurice, 133
Shand, Captain, 61
Shaw Savill & Albion Co, 50–51, 56, 58, 79, 97
Shell Oil, 104
Shrimski, Samuel, 34
Short, Captain, Thomas, 23
ships: 222, 88; Adventure, 125; Anne, 25; Anne Jane, 19; Aorangi, 131; Aorea, 77; Aramoana, 109; Ardentinny, 139; Ata, 106–07; A.W. Stevens, 25; Awanui,112-113 141; Banshee, 27, 142; Beautiful Star, 22, 36, 45, 53, 63; Bellona, HMNZS, 140; Breeze, 103–04; Brisk, 142; Brunner, 67; Border Knight, 69; Calm, 110–11; Canadian Tide, 114-115; Canterbury, 93; Caroline, 28–29, 142; Chieftain, 53; Claribel, 53; Claverdon, 69; Coptic, 97; Coquette, 25; Cora, 142; Corinna, 83; Dagmar, 22; Duke of Westminster, 72; Dunedin, 52–53, 59; Elderslie (sailing ship), 41, 143; Elderslie (steamer), 52–55; Emile, 143; Empire Dirk, 99; Emu, 29, 31; Emulous, 26–27, 143; Endeavour, 18; Essex, 72; Fanny, 143; Fifeshire, 72, 144; Fly, 142; Franklin Belle, 46, 143; Friendship, 144; Frysna, 107; Gazehound, 142; Geelong, 21, 27, 45; Good Templar, 46; Hawea, 60, 63; Highlander, 28, 142; Hinemoa, 63–65; Holmburn, 106, 109; Holmdale, 88; Holmdale (1961), 106,113-114; Holmglen, 104–06; Holmlea, 109; Holmwood, 11, 108; Hope, 25, 27, 142; Hotunui, 106, 141; Inverell, HMNZS, 119; Jane, 143; Kaikoura, 85–87; Kaiwaka, 121, Kanna, 11, 102, 109; Kakapo, 140; Karamea, 83; Karetu, 113; Kauri, 102, 141; Kent, 90; Kiwi, HMNZS, 126; Konini, 109; Koputai, 53; Koraki, 141; Kotare, 83; John, 83; Lobo, 79; Mamari, 58; Maori (USSCo), 21–22; Maori (SS&ACo) 45; Marlborough, 55; Margaret Campbell, 143; Margaret Galbraith, 67; Mary Ann Christina, 34; Mary Ogilvie, 143; Matau, 41; Mercia, 53; Midlothian, 25, 27, 142; Min Tide, 114; Moa, HMNZS, 126; Moura, 80; Nairnshire, 58; Ngamotu, 114; Ngatoro, 84; Oamaru Lass (later Nora); 22, 142; Ocean Wave, 27, 143; Onehunga, 143; Opawa, 88, 94–95; Oriti, 143; Otago, 29, 31, 142; Otaio, 88–89, 94–95; Otakou, 99; Our Hope, 143; Papanui, 77; Paparoa, 85; Pareora, 72; Parera, 108, 114; Pirate, 21; Pleiades, 56–57; Plucky, 63; Port Dunedin, 83; Premier, 23, 143; Progress, 52–53, 60, 62, 75–77, 79, 82, 139–40; Pukeko, 106, 114-15; Queen, 21; Rakaia, 73, 75; Raranga, 88; Reynolds, 64–65; Richard and Mary, 143; Rimutaka, 88; Ringarooma, HMS, 58; Ringdove, HMS, 58; Robert and Betsy, 22, 30, 142; Royal Bride, 22–23; Samson, 41, 45; Scotsman, 143; Silver Cloud, 67; Spec, 19; Somerset, 97, 140; Spithead, 69; Stately, 25; Star, 19; Star of Tasmania (schooner), 22, 142; Star of Tasmania (ship), 25, 29–31, 142; Star of Victoria, 69; Stately, 142; Storm, 106, 108, 113–14; Swordfish, 47; Tainui, 106; Tanea, 103–04, 141; Tararua, 22; Tarawera, 80–81; Tekapo, 60–61; Tekoa, 70–71; Terra Nova, 12, 84; Thomas and Henry, 20, 29; Turakina (sailing ship), 69; Turakina (steamer) 96–97, 140; Turihaua, 103; Unicorn, 58; Unit Shipper, 113; United Brothers, 143; Van Cloon, 98; Vistula, 25–26, 142; Vixen, 23, 25, 142; Vulcan, 125; Waimea, 112; Waimate, 83; Wainui, 27; Waipa, 56–57; Waipahi, 102–03; Waitaki, 43, 45; Waiwera, 73–75; Wakatipu, 56–57, 67; Wallace, 21–22, 24, 27, 45; Wanaka, 83; Water Nymph, 29–31, 142; Wellington, 22, 142; Werneth Hall, 69; Westmorland, 88; W.H. Orbell, 109, 141; Whitehead Bay, HMS Willem Barendsz 115,140; William and Jane, 48; Yuho Maru, 98–99; Zealandic, 97
slipways, 92, 124–5, 140–41
Smedley, Bill, 100
Stannes family, 85
Star & Garter Hotel, 57, 59, 73
Stephens, Win, 100
Stevens, Mr, 30–31
Sumpter, Beatrice, 49
Sumpter, George, 46, 49, 66
Surf Bay, 93, 98, 123
Surfboats, see landing service
Sutherland, W., 85

SWAG (Sumpter Wharf Action Group), 137
swimming, 92, 101

Tangney, Ian Paul, 122, 125
Tangney, Syd, 18, 124–25
tetrapods, 7, 99, 127–29
Thomson, Captain William, 32
Todd, Rev. Alexander, 137
Todd, G.W., 137
Traill, Charles, 20
Traill, Roxby & Co, 25, 31
tugs and barges, 113
Turnbull, Martin & Co, 52

Union Steam Ship Co of New Zealand, 45,
    57, 60, 67, 79–81, 99, 106, 109, 114

Vogel, Julius, 25, 42
Voss, Captain John, 70

Waimate County Council, 120
Waitaki County Council, 120
Waitaki District Council, 123–23, 127–28,
    131, 137
Walkem & Peyman, 38–39
Wanbrow, Cape, 16–17; 34, 72; 124
Wansbeck Street footbridge, 72
Ward, A., 59
Ward, E., 59
Wards, Ian, 35
Warner Pacific Line, 106–07
Warren, Arthur, 67
Waterfront Industry Commission, 100, 102,
    104
Waterside workers ('wharfies'), 67, 102–05
Watson, A., 66
wildlife: shags, 12–13; blue penguins
    131–32; seals, 132
Williams, Cyrus, 89–90
Williams, Captain Henry, 104
Wilson, Edward, 84
Wilson, Ron, 122
Winders, Pat and John, 124
wharves: 1867 jetty, 25, 28, 31, 139;
    Macandrew Wharf, 41–45, 127, 134, 139;
    Normanby Wharf, 43, 44–45, 111; Cross
    Wharf, 10, 46, 49, 135–36, 139; Sumpter
    Wharf, 12–13, 50–51, 53, 55–58, 66,
    69–73, 80–81, 94, 117, 121, 132, 136–37,
    139; Holmes Wharf, 9, 73, 79, 81, 88–89,
    94–95, 106–07, 113–14, 116, 122–23, 136,
    139–41; Dredging Jetty, 140; North
    Otago Yacht & Power Boat Club Jetties,
    141
Whitson, Captain, 53–54
World Heritage List, 134
Worst Journey in the World, 84
wrecks/marine occurrences, 22–23, 25–29;
    46, 104–06, 142–44; see also specific
    vessels

yachting, see recreational boating
Young, Duncan, 30

On weekends the Oamaru Steam and Rail Restoration Society's steam train runs from Itchen Street down to the Red Sheds by Normanby Wharf. A Rogers locomotive, K92, was on loan to the Society in 2007–08. – Gavin McLean

Acknowledgements

This book began with a discussion in Oamaru between Otago University Press and Take Note bookshop after the launch of *How To Do Local History* in February 2007. I have for many years been writing about colonial Oamaru's heritage, the harbour especially, and I thank them for allowing me the opportunity to reflect again on that history, this time through a heritage lens, inspired in part by Erik Olssen and Tom Field's splendid *Relics of the Goldfields*.

In Oamaru, I thank the North Otago Museum staff, past and present, for access to the collection on several occasions and for helpful suggestions about sources: Jon Brocas, Rowan Carroll, Thomas Heyes, Bruce McCulloch, Kathleen Stringer and Ian Wards. Councillors Rodney Grater and Helen Stead were always interested in promoting the town's history and heritage. At the Oamaru Whitestone Civic Trust, Warwick and Faye Ormondy kept me abreast of developments and supplied a copy of the Sumpter Wharf conservation plan. I also thank Waitaki District Council CE, Michael Ross, for his comments.

I also thank Captain A. Grieve of Pleasant Point, former harbour master, who commented on a draft of chapter 6, and to Lawrence Hardy from the WDC, who talked about his decade as honorary harbour master, and to Graeme Ferris, 'waterfront stone-kicker', who talked about the place and who generously lent photographs. For additional photography I thank Heather Mathie and Marian Minson of the Alexander Turnbull Library in Wellington, Grant Seath of Tauranga, and Ian Farquhar of Dunedin. Once again Kynan Gentry of Wellington's digital jiggery-pokery breathed new life into some very tired old images.

Primary sources

The North Otago Museum holds the records of the Oamaru Dock Trust, Oamaru Harbour Board and the Harbour Committee of the Oamaru Borough Council and later of the Waitaki District Council. The holding is extensive and very complete. In addition to these records, I also used the Harbour Association of New Zealand files held by the Alexander Turnbull Library, miscellaneous ships' logs and other material held by the same institution, and the Marine Department, Railways, Treasury, Audit and records on Oamaru held by Archives New Zealand. Full references are in the end notes.

Secondary sources

The main book on the harbour history is my *Oamaru Harbour: Port in a Storm* (Dunmore Press, Palmerston North, 1982) and my chapter 'Tides of History: Oamaru Harbour' in Kynan Gentry and Gavin McLean (eds), *Heartlands: New Zealand Historians Write About Where History Happened* (Penguin, Auckland, 2006). For a general background to Oamaru history, see K.C. McDonald, *White Stone Country* (Dunedin, 1962) and McDonald (edited by Gavin McLean), *Oamaru 1878: A Colonial Town* (1878 Publication Group of the Waitaki District Council, Oamaru, 2006). Conal McCarthy's *Forrester and Lemon of Oamaru, Architects* (North Otago Branch Committee of the New Zealand Historic Places Trust, Oamaru, 2002) examines the architectural legacy of the harbour board's talented secretary.

For a background to New Zealand maritime history, see David Johnson, *New Zealand's Maritime Heritage* (Collins/David Bateman, Auckland, 1987) and Gavin McLean, *Captain's Log: New Zealand Maritime History* (Hodder Moa Beckett, Auckland, 2001). Two books from Otago Heritage Books of Dunedin illuminate aspects of Otago's maritime history: Ian Church, *Opening the Manifest on Otago's Infant Years: Shipping Arrivals and Departures, Otago Harbour and Coast 1770–1860* (2002) and Bruce Collins, *Rocks, Reefs and Sandbars: A History of Otago Shipwrecks* (1995).